Each of these pieces of handwriting is by a well-known person. See how many you can identify!
At the end of the book you'll find the names of the people together with a character reading of their writing by a graphologist.

This space is for a piece of your natural handwriting.

...think of my handwriting.

Mad dogs and Englishmen go out in the midday sun.

My Auntie flo's got a big nose, or so it said, cos auntie flos dead.

of sand

pain

...in Igmorant you stupid

...will come to all of us

...ill not be there to see it.

go handwriting a key to character

Once upon a time there were two chinamen. Now look how many there are!

A rose can only be just a rose but you are you

When a guy opens a car door for a girl, either the car is new or the girl is!

England Rules! See You Soon

Hello! How are yo...

Er well thanks a lot, but I'd rather go on me own like!
A walk in the air is something you may dare when you've had to much to drink but don't take a chance on driving your car because its highly, nighly you'll find yourself in clink.

interested of this is 2...

Mat

The quick brown fox jumped over the lazy dog.

What's your bag, man?

I will drink the wine while it is warm and never let you catch me looking at the su...

Would anyone like to buy a second hand Japanese motorised replica of Jack Lancaster?

...thought less about politics & religion... more about humanity the world would... happier place.

...were playing holiday... be as tedious as... to work (statefu...

Joe played Tobin in 'the Knack' twice Why?

"All that glitters is not gold".

When the Sufi is using his intuition, he... explain his actions plausibly. The s... also gives the possessor of BARAKA t... apparently to create certain he...

12/6

FAB GANG 1971

This is the laughing, stamping, taping, writing, clicking, snapping, drawing, designing, persuading crowd of people who put this book together. It's the same team that gets together FAB 208 each week. In detail, we are: (starting at the top, l. to r.) Richard Stone (chief sub), Derek Reeve (art room), John Hamon (letterbox), Lorraine Guest (girl Friday), Sue Coath (production), Brian Thomas (art ed.), Lorraine Wright (letterbox), Sarah Parkin (art room), Mia Scammel (fashion asst), Georgina Mells (writer), Betty Hale (ed.), Heather Kirby (fashion ed.), Janet Kaye (art room), Jocelyn Morton (pic ed.), Julia Einhorn (asst art ed.), Judith Wills (writer).

Call it a Decade of Drama. Or Ten Years of Triumph. For that is the life-span of the wonderful Beatles. From riot-raising in the noisy city of Hamburg back in 1961, to their current headline-hogging status round the whole world . . . Ten Top Pop Years.

As the Swinging Sixties got under way, the Beatles were very much a team. Now, as the Storming Seventies push ahead, they lead individual lives but still make mind-shattering music.

As individuals, Paul, John, George and Ringo have obviously changed over the years. Let's look closely at how those changes have come about.

JOHN LENNON, the gruff voice, both on and off-stage. Rhythm guitarist. The biggest Beatle, size-wise, and probably talent-wise, too. Back in 1961, John was a conversational grunter. And he put on a fixed glare sometimes that put the fear of the unknown into many an interviewer. Actually the glare came because he was very short-sighted, but didn't like the idea of wearing glasses!

Still, looking back, John was the one who first got fed up with constant questioning.

"Who the heck cares whether I wear pyjamas in bed, or eat cornflakes at breakfast?" he'd grunt. But people DID care and they kept asking.

John didn't suffer fools gladly. "He needs a punch on the nose to liven him up," he'd say in that deep voice of his. And there wasn't any sign of a smile. Sure, he came out with the occasional wisecrack—he'd somehow save it up, then chuck it out into the conversation at precisely the right moment.

Back in the 1962, '63, '64 era, as things really hummed for the Beatles, John was definitely the aggressive, almost war-like Beatle. He looked and sounded as if he could be very violent indeed. Often he opened his mouth and, to coin a phrase, put his foot in it. "The Beatles are more popular now than Jesus Christ," said he in 1966. The result: headlines all round the world, most of them hammering poor John.

Poor John? Well, he knew and the others knew that it was all a mistake. At that time, he had difficulty getting his quick-silver thoughts out in the right words. What he meant was that there was something wrong with a world which put a rock and roll group up on a pedestal and yet produced only tiny congregations in the churches.

The criticism really wounded John. Even then he was saying that he wouldn't be able to put up with the life of a Beatle for much longer. . . .

He'd been soured, too, by the spotlight put upon his wife Cynthia and their son Julian. Those of us close to the Beatles knew he was married but John had begged us to say nothing. "They say it'll spoil the image," he growled. "But that's not it. I just want them to be able to lead a private life."

Again, he'd been misjudged. He was accused of deliberately trying to hide the truth. "But they just didn't ask me about a wife," he said. And he was right.

In those early days, John had a grasshopper mind. He started finding an interest in different religions, but only to see what was wrong with him. But the war-like Beatle really changed during his spell of transcendental meditation under the guidance of the bearded Indian mystic, the Maharishi.

He has said his "new" life began when he met up with Yoko Ono. Together they set out on a collision course with the world over matters like peace and understanding.

He became a sort of crank, always involved in stunts. His "lie-ins" in the cause of peace, his appearance with Yoko in huge white bags, his sending of acorns to the world leaders—all natural headline stories and not all taken as seriously as John wanted.

Certainly the hardest Beatle to get to know, John's mind right now is bulging with ideas for his life over the next ten years. Could be politics, or his own kind of religion—but it'd have to be HIS scene.

His toughness still shows in his music—he's the rocker Beatle, both in his songs and in his *Twist and Shout* type rave-ups. But the peaceful side is what shows in his off-duty life.

He's changed from being un-complicated and blunt to being complex on a spiritual level. Which is not what we expected in those days back in 1961 and 1962.

PAUL McCARTNEY, the polite and soft voice, both on and off-stage. Left-handed bassist. The youngest Beatle but the quickest to mature and come to terms with pop music.

While John Lennon was glaring, back in the early Beatle days, Paul was doing a good public relations job. With the face of an angelic choirboy, he'd make strangers welcome in the dressing-rooms of the world—but nobody could possibly have taken him for an easy touch.

All the same, he wanted to help. He wanted the Beatles to become the biggest thing ever and his ambition forced him to be nice to the right people. Yet over the years, his sense of humour has gone from the impish to the hard-hitting.

Paul kept his interest going longer than the others. At one stage, while John, George and Ringo were dreaming up excuses to get out of engagements, there was Paul having business lunches, going to receptions, being seen around—and literally forcing the others to show some vitality at the photographic sessions which were an everyday part of the Beatle life.

There was his long-standing romance with Jane Asher. It ended abruptly, but they were happy days generally and there was nothing Paul could do to keep it out of the papers. Paul was artistic and Paul was the main sex symbol within the group—he knew he photographed well and even the hard life of touring failed to change the smooth complexion and the clear-white of his eyes.

We all thought he'd marry early because domesticity appealed to him so much. In fact, he held out for years. Then came a whirlwind romance with the lovely Linda. And the real changes followed—inevitable though they obviously were.

While the others had made plans for country houses and whatever privacy they could find, Paul didn't mind at all living close to the centre of London. He enjoyed the live-it-up life . . . until Linda finally emerged to offer him the family, round-the-hearth sort of life that he'd always wanted.

So Paul became something of a recluse, living way up in the wilds of Scotland and behaving very tersely indeed with photographers and reporters who managed to track him down. When he did go to London, for recording sessions, he did so quietly. He left behind his pets and animals and really regretted being caught up in the hectic life of London.

What's more his resentment tended to show. There were disputes between him and John, where before there had been only a sort of telepathic matiness. Paul had taken longest to crack

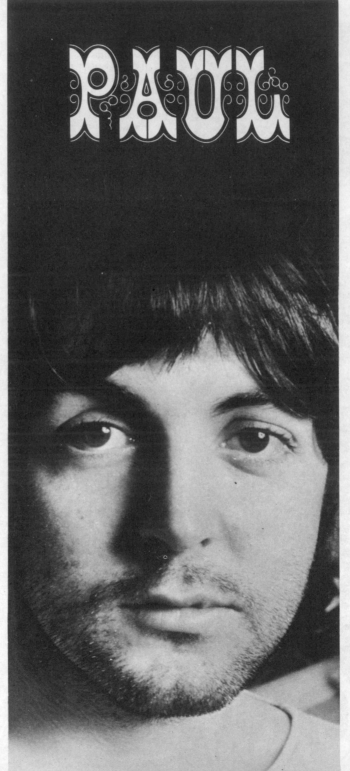

and re-act against the goldfish-type of life the Beatles had led, but when he DID crack you could almost hear the noise all over the pop world.

However, in one respect, Paul hasn't changed. He still gets kicks out of the simple things of life. Listen to him describing a holiday in Greece or the West Indies . . . he re-lives every moment, describes scenery with a sort of awe-inspired reverence. It's not an act. Not even years of hard-living and tough-travelling have dampened his excitement at seeing new places. Or meeting new people.

While the others needed close organisation to get them through a working day, Paul organised himself with ruthless efficiency. He'd snap at bad service or poor time-keeping but he is still quite fantastic at making friends with little children. Sometimes he's got very angry indeed when he thinks that George or John have damaged the Beatle image, but he never lets them down in public by "leaking" his complaints to the newspapermen.

Though he had a bad spell around 1966, Paul has probably been the most popular Beatle in the fringe areas of pop music. And that is because he has plenty to say for himself and for his future, even if he rarely comes out with anything controversial.

It's easy to say that Paul now is not quite as nice a character as he was in the early days. But then consider the enormous strain under which he has been living. One thing, though : don't let that angelic, cute face fool you into thinking that there are positively NO skeletons in his personal cupboard.

Back in those raving, but pretty anonymous days in Germany, Paul was the master-mind of some stunts that shook the daylights even out of the tolerant hard-living Germans. Not the sort of things one can write about, unfortunately, but real eye-openers for all that.

Friendly, uncomplicated, but hardening up as the years go by . . . that's Paul. In touch with reality as opposed to fantasy—which is how he writes the most commercial songs.

GEORGE HARRISON, lead guitarist, thin and thoughtful, surely the best musician in the group. A mixture of nice 'n' nasty, even in those early days in Germany. George more or less created the hard-driving sounds that made the Beatles world favourites.

He's the Memory Man of the Beatles, even now. He looks back happily, says: "Germany was great. We played long hours and the management would say: "Make Schtomp", which meant banging our feet on the stage and really getting a beat going. . . ."

At that time, and right through to 1966, George enjoyed the touring. More even than the others. But it was he who finally put the block on the Beatles making further concert appearances. He even walked out of a recording session, having argued that touring was a backward step—and it was him, driving off angrily, that caused the others to change their ideas.

Friends figured that George was, for a long time, the least affected of the Beatles. But he's always been a sensitive soul, has George. He felt the strain, even if he didn't let it show. Marriage to Pattie Boyd helped him settle down a bit, but he gradually grew less and less tolerant of the characters who uselessly hung around the Beatle scene.

Without going out of his way to be pushy, George was helpful and co-operative. But once he felt the old-style Beatlemania was over, he chucked in the towel. He resented questions about his personal life . . . sought peace in his study of the Eastern religions and cults. As for Indian music . . . well, he proved his musicianship by learning to play the sitar, one of the hardest instruments in the world.

No dabbler, George. At first, just hard rock and roll was his fancy. But when he turned to Indian sounds, he turned completely. He studied every aspect. Because with George, if a thing is worth doing, then it was to be done well.

Strangely enough, George was a good sportsman at school. He ran, played cricket, soccer—even then, he wouldn't turn out for a game unless he felt he would do well. Maybe that's why he turned so much against personal appearances . . . "We were the biggest attraction, so why go back to something we know we do well."

He grew the first Beatle beard, later trimming it back to a mere moustache. Otherwise, his personal appearance hasn't changed much over the years—just a few extra pounds of flesh here and there.

Certainly he has changed more than the others. Where just playing guitar well was his main ambition—he'd sit, polishing his instrument through the longest of interviews, clearly in love with its shape and feel—now he's turned into a most imaginative producer. His music for the film *Wonderwall* opened up a whole new area of work, because George had, as a composer, been so long in the shadows of Paul and John.

He nurses his own talent along, spending hours and hours in the studios coaxing the very best sounds. It's as if he no longer feels he wants to show himself off to the public—he wants respect on a higher creative level than just flashing that old slow-burning toothy smile.

And he introduced the Radna Krishna Temple to an unsuspecting public. The International Society for Krishna Consciousness trained people in self-purification in order to find out how to love their spiritual master. George was fascinated with the Eastern links. He'd thought of joining but one Temple rule was not to touch stimulants—George had long since given up spirits and wine, but he reckoned he couldn't live without cigarettes or coffee.

But he added: "It's one way to help people find God. We are all looking for a peaceful world . . . maybe this is one way."

Yes, George searches on for the answer to world conflict. But in a quieter, more personalised way than the spectacular efforts of John Lennon.

Once George said: "The Beatles? . . . well, it's not the living end, is it!" Which is his way of getting things in the right order. Could be that the generally amiable George is just a shade too honest for the phoney side of pop. A tremendous talent, of course, and there's a lot more brilliance yet to come from his alert mind.

GEORGE

If George now has a few thousand acquaintances, he definitely has few friends. He likes it that way. He's more aware about money than the others, much more so now than in the early days when he regarded a pay-packet as merely containing something which would buy him more guitars.

When George speaks, he speaks slowly. But you can trust implicity what he says. Therein lies his essential niceness over ten harassing years.

RINGO STARR, drummer, clown, the only Beatle to have changed his real name (Richard Starkey) to suit the pop world. The oldest Beatle, the smallest Beatle, the newest Beatle.

Of course, Ringo has changed. He's discovered that there are other vegetables than chipped potatoes, for instance. He's been through his big-spending years, though, when he'd lavish large sums of money round the clubs of London—and he's pretty well back where he started. A now-wealthy character who happens to enjoy life at home and sees no need at all to live it up in the accepted star manner.

Still, Ringo started off with a bit of a handicap. While the other Beatles were roaring round Hamburg, with a Liverpudlian named Pete Best on drums, Ringo had his own group (earning thirty bob a night) and also worked in a Butlin holiday camp.

It was decided that Ringo should be called in on drums around the time of the very first single, *Love Me Do*. When that disc hit the charts, Ringo was there for all the Press conferences but, because he was so new to the scene, he did little of the talking. He had the eyes of a clown, a nose which made him a bit self-conscious, and he looked so small and vulnerable.

Those who took the trouble to talk to him found him helpful and courteous. But mostly he was quiet and withdrawn. In the background on stage, he stayed right there when the group was not actually working. Pity more journalists didn't spend time with him in the early days, because Ringo was generally good for a few amusing quotes.

Ringo's marriage to Maureen Cox, and the family they created, gave him all the basic roots he needed. He never has rated himself as a drummer, reckoning he's adequate but that's all. In *Help* he showed he could have a future as a film comedian and, being less dedicated to music than John, Paul or George, he went on a solo career which took in the movies *Candy* and *Magic Christian*.

In the very early days, Ringo suffered a lot mentally because there were demonstrations against him in Liverpool from fans of Pete Best. That also drove him into his shell. It took Ringo longer than the others to get accustomed to fame and he was genuinely shy and amused when, for a while, American fans rated him the most popular Beatle of all! "Oh, shurrup", he'd say as the others read juicy items about him from fan magazines ...

He also said: "I'm two people. Richard Starkey and Ringo Starr. Ringo can look after himself at last, not like in the first years of travelling with the Beatles. Then, I didn't know what was happening. I was more a spectator in a way."

When the others agreed that touring and concert dates were out, Ringo went along with the decision but he still reckons he'd like to get back on stage. There is a lot of the showman even in the Ringo of today and he has easily the most expressive face of all Beatles.

Ringo once said: "Because of illness, I missed out on a lot of schooling and I suppose it gave me a kind of inferiority complex. Then, with the Beatles, I found I had to learn to live in a big-money world and I couldn't make excuses for anything—I had to learn to cope. In that sense, it's been a really helpful career, apart from the bread I've made."

Ringo wants his sons to have the very best of life but at the same time to learn to stand on their own feet. He's absolutely devoted to Maureen and the boys and that explains the long periods when he has been out of the public eye.

The future for Ringo? Hard to say. He has these spasms when he gets fed up with the boredom of doing little. He feels he has little talent as a songwriter, not much interest in production and is not entirely convinced by the fans who reckon he has a very good singing voice.

"I suppose it'll be just me," he says. "I enjoy acting—maybe that is the answer. I like making my own movies at home, but that doesn't mean I see myself as a big-time director. I just don't know."

Ringo's ten years have been very much up and down. Down at first when he didn't look like having much of a future in music ... then up when he joined, out of the blue, the Beatles.

In 1961, he found it hard to relax. Now he's come to terms with his status and his comfortable home life enables him to feel perfectly clear of the stresses and strains.

Ringo, basically, has changed less than the others. But as he says: "You can't have been a Beatle without changing a lot. Better ask all of us how we feel in, say, ten years' time!"

MARK DAY

HAVE YOU GOT WHAT IT TAKES?

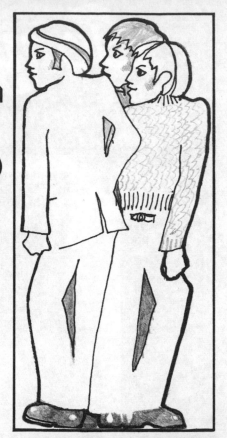

A lucky few are born with it, that certain something that makes men flock around, from the crib to the rocking chair, but the rest of us are naturally without and learning fast. Find out which you are.

1

You go to a dance with a very pretty friend. What happens?
a) She meets a smashing boy and you go home alone.
b) You meet brothers and yours is the good-looking one.
c) You dance with each other all evening.

2

You are invited to dinner at the Post Office Tower and you're crazy about him but you hate heights. Do you?
a) Say you're busy and hope he asks you again somewhere more down-to-earth.
b) Explain you hate heights but would love to go somewhere else.
c) Accept and either wear dark glasses or determine to have such a good time you forget where you are but not who you're with.

3

You travel each morning on the train/bus with a gorgeous boy. Do you?
a) Regularly fight your way to the seat next to him and then bury yourself in a varied series of interesting books so that he has a chance to ask if you're interested in beekeeping or medieval wall-hangings too.
b) Get up half an hour earlier in the mornings so you always look your best when you see him and after several weeks without apparently noticing him use an unexpected sudden stop as an excuse to fall into his lap.
c) Tell yourself all he's interested in is getting to his stop, that he probably has a girlfriend already, and that you're wasting your time, so forget it.

4

Do you?
a) Always wear clean, unladdered tights.
b) Never have chipped varnish or chewed nails.
c) Have a bath every day.
d) Smile and look happy more often than not.

5

You were last invited and went to a party . . . (ones you didn't attend don't count)
a) Last week.
b) Last month.
c) Last year.

6

The exotic dish you order in a restaurant turns out to be calves' brains and cooked celery and you can't stand either. Do you?
a) Grin and bear it while you swill the lot down with too much wine.
b) Admit your ignorance and ask for a small omelette instead.
c) Eat a little and then say you're too happy to eat.

7

He asks you to the local amateur dramatics production and your ex-boyfriend has the leading part. Do you?
a) Boo loudly and often.
b) Clap politely and leave promptly.
c) Rave about how good he was.

8

Your wardrobe includes:
a) One maxi or midi.
b) A wig that's a different colour to your own hair.
c) A chain belt but not gilt or gold.

9

You are at the cinema and it's a tragic love story and you forgot your hankie. Do you?
a) Sniff.
b) Ask if you can borrow his, and make it seem like a romantic thing to do.
c) Rush to the loo and see if there's anywhere you can buy or borrow a tissue.

10

You walk into a room that's mostly full of strangers. Do you?
a) Look around desperately for any vaguely familiar face.
b) Drop your bracelet and wait for six people to rush to help you put it back on.
c) Walk straight up to the dishiest man there and say "How super to see you again".

11

When your last romance finished . . . ?
a) You considered you were better off without him and found someone new within a week.
b) You moped around for days saying there'd never be anyone like him again in your life.
c) Your last romance never started.

12

Do you usually spend your evenings?
a) At home alone.
b) With girlfriends enjoying yourself.
c) Out with a boy.
d) Out with friends but not really having a good time and wishing you were with a boy.

Georgina Mells

(*Turn to page 75 for your score and rating.*)

9

Tony Blackburn says-

Somewhere in the heart of London, a few minutes from the BBC, Tony
Blackburn leaps out of bed every weekday at 5 a.m. to rush off and broadca

Tony's pride and joy is his video-tape machine, along with his record player, tape recorder and colour tele.

*This is the Blackburn bed where Tony snores the nights away. His idea of heaven is to go to bed by ten and doze in front
of the portable tele. Comes of having to get up at the crack of dawn.*

come on over to my place

his show. But this hectic way of life has its compensations - like a super-comfortable, luxury flat where he can really relax after a morning's work.

Tony busy making a cup of tea in his luxury, ultra-efficient kitchen—and very good it tasted too.

Apart from his morning show Tony has a very busy diary of engagements —like compering "Top of the Pops" and judging beauty competitions— not that he ever complains about those !

He likes to have friends in quite often, and with those super-comfortable chairs to sink into, a stack of records to listen to, and an endless supply of tea, we bet they hope they get invited again.

Emma's Pets Pad

Emma, the black and white cat, is one of the regular stars of FAB. She and Toby (who is also black and white and furry) both live happily with Christine Osbourne now — but once they were strays, with no place of their own. This is what Chris thinks Emma would like to say, if cats could talk . . .

Christmas and Summer holidays are the times the animal sanctuaries dread the most. They're the times the animals stream in. The old cat, terrified, dumped on the clinic table with a curt "Put it down". Dogs, abandoned on busy streets while their family—all they've ever known—drive casually off with the holiday cases piled in the back. Left to sit bewildered on the pavement until somebody cares, or to run panic-stricken among the traffic until a car hits them and it's too late. Unwanted, shoved aside, because it's holiday time and they're going away and boarding kennels cost money whereas dumping, or having an animal put down costs nothing.

Two weeks after Christmas is another time. It's the puppies and the kittens this time, the kitten who laddered a pair of tights, the puppy who puddled on the floor, or perhaps it was simply that the novelty wore off. Puppies and kittens are lovely presents to give. Warm and cuddly, appealing—and not nearly as expensive as a teddy bear. And then the oohs and aahs stop and in they come. Lonely, dejected, bewildered, unhappy. Don't ever give an animal as a present unless you've made sure it will be wanted. And before you take in a pet yourself—have a little think.

A dog will cost you anything from ten bob to a couple of quid depending on his size and how you feed him. A cat should be able to live like a queen on ten bob unless they're the Emma and Toby sort who are too darn fussy. But it isn't the money, it's time. This really applies to dogs as cats—although they love a lot of attention and a good old fuss—are very self sufficient. Your dog needs your company. It's no good leaving him on his own all day in the garden with a quick walk morning and night. He won't be happy—and you won't get so much out of your relationship with him either. And incidentally, it's the bored dog who strips the wallpaper off the walls, dines off your best sheepskin slippers and chews through the table leg while you're having tea.

Cats cause virtually no damage at all—neither of ours have apart from the odd accident.

All animals bring in vet's bills—and not just the sick ones. You must have your puppy inoculated against distemper, cats against feline enteritis. Also, it is essential to have your pet doctored. This is something I personally found very difficult. I don't like the idea of taking away an animal's masculinity or femininity. But when you think that each year, thousands of stray animals roam the streets, end up at an animal sanctuary, or are humanely destroyed, you know that if you care anything at all about animals, it has to be done.

Then there's house training. Kittens are rarely any problem—they're incredible really, even at six weeks, mum will have told them what it's all about. Puppies aren't so bright in this respect, it will take a couple of months more—if you stay calm, gentle and firm. It is cruel to shout at a puppy, hit him, try to bully him into doing what you want. And you lose in the end—he'll take longer to learn and he will fear instead of love you.

One other thing, if you live in a flat, do make sure pets are allowed first. Don't take in an animal, grow to love it and it you, and then have to sit back and watch it join that sad stream of the unwanted.

Cilla and Bobby Willis are two people who have gone about things in just the right way. They're both dog-lovers and the proud owners of two Briards called Sophie and Ada. It's a rare breed in this country—which I can best describe as a French sheepdog—and they cost £135 each. Weekly food bill is around six pounds and because Cilla and Bobby are both busy people, they're frequently out exercising the dogs at two in the morning. At the time of going to press they were busy looking for a big house with a nice big garden specially because they happen to be responsible for two very large dogs!

But Cilla and Bobby thought all this over before they got the dogs so they're happy. And so incidentally are Sophie and Ada.

And so . . . choose the pet you can afford. Feed him properly, remembering that overfeeding is even worse than underfeeding. An old dog that's lean is generally healthy. A fat old dog puffs, pants and has a thoroughly miserable time. Make sure you're prepared to do the dirty jobs too—like cleaning out a rabbit's cage. Don't ever leave a dog alone all day to fret and pine.

And one last thing, keep your eye on other people's pets. If you see a dog chained up day after day, or knocked about, or half starved—reach for that phone and tell your local RSPCA inspector. You may stop some unspeakable cruelty.

I know it's an awful thought that Mr. Thingummy up the road who's been kicking his dog with hobnailed boots and feeding him one bone per day may come and punch you on the nose. It won't happen because he wouldn't ever be given your name.

A woman came up to me last week and told me about two big dogs being kept in a small shed, on a very short chain with no light. "It's disgusting . . . he knocks them around. Someone should do something about it," this dog-lover told me, her face pink with indignation at the cruelty. I asked her why she hadn't done anything.

She hadn't wanted her name involved.

Don't be like that even if it does take a bit of courage. Because, in this respect at least, animals really are dumb.

Christine Osbourne

DEAD OR ALIVE IN POP

BY KEITH ALTHAM

Do you remember the old original Amen Corner, Love Affair, Herd, Small Faces and the Bonzo Dogs? Was there ever an era when groups formed and re-formed with such regularity? We try to keep you abreast of the present line-ups but by the time you read this they may have all had yet another reshuffle!

1969
YEAR OF CHANGES

It was the Year of the "Changes" for British beat groups as they re-shuffled their line-ups, splintered into break away units or simply faded into obscurity in the desperate attempt to find new directions.

'SCREAMAGERS'

The day of the walking talking singing ten by eight glossy were numbered and as the screamagers began to dwindle, a more mature and listenable era dawned led largely by the great gods "BeatleStones" who set the pattern switching their music from the hearts to the heads.

'BEATLESTONES'

SMALL FACES HUMBLE PIE

One of the first groups into the great "now you see them now you don't" syndrome were the Small Faces who lost Steve Marriott to the group which also claimed Peter Frampton of the Herd and became Humble Pie, Steve explained to reporters that he was tired of being what he called a "teen-scream" and wanted to get into that "heavier" category who would listen.

'TEEN-SCREAM'

"The Faces were a gas to begin with and we all played for each other but after a while we turned into something we were not," says Steve. "People began to look upon me as a lead guitarist which I have never been and we were reduced to playing our old hits night after night. The best thing to happen for both of us was my leaving."

'THE FACE OF '68'
PETER FRAMPTON

Peter Frampton who was branded "The Face of '68" affirms Steve's view that you must divide to conquer.

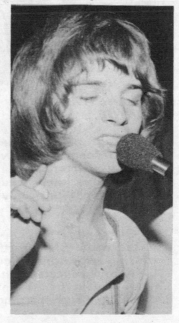

"Up to six months before I joined the Herd I had never sung a note in my life," says Peter. "I was a guitarist who felt like he had his hands tied behind his back. Now I'm doing what I do best with Humble Pie—playing guitar."

THE CREAM

Perhaps the strangest break-up in pop has been that of the Cream who splintered into Blind Faith which in turn became Airforce for a short time, The original members of the Cream considered by many still to have been the finest example of "super-rock" were Ginger Baker, Jack Bruce and ace guitarist Eric Clapton, who explained the reasons for the Cream clotting thus!

'SUPER-ROCK'

Continued from page 13

"It just became a very heavy virtuoso scene," says Eric. "We were each getting into long solo instrumental passages on stage beginning to turn out music which could only be created in a recording studio. We were not contributing anything to the unit as a whole and lost our joy in being live musicians!"

BLIND FAITH

And so it was that Blind Faith came to be last year which included Clapton and Baker from the Cream set-up plus the vocal multi-instrumental talents of Stevie Winwood and that of a relative newcomer Rick Gretch who played bass and violin. Faith made one rhapsodised appearance for free in Hyde Park—a tour of America —produced an album which soared to number one in the best selling LP charts on both sides of the Atlantic and then mysteriously appeared to disappear up their own amplifiers! A large question mark now hangs over that group's future especially since Ginger Baker's brief excursion with his superband which featured Stevie Winwood and Clapton's musical flirtation with Delaney and Bonnie.

DELANEY AND BONNIE

A disgruntled Ginger Baker informed, following the Airforce tour, that no one knew what was happening about Faith.

"Originally it was supposed to be Blind Faith touring with Bonnie and Delaney," revealed Ginger. "But when I got back he was helping them out on his own so we put Airforce together. Airforce is not considered a permanent thing either—it's just a now and again band. We don't seem to be able to do permanent things."

ONO BAND

Clapton continued in his generous musical outlook of having a guitar for hire to friends like Lennon and the Ono band and just where anyone goes from there is debateable. It maybe that the temporary nature of groups like Faith and Airforce is more a deliberate policy by musicians now than is understood and the Jimi Hendrix Experience appear to have gone the way of this "anything goes" format.

JIMI HENDRIX

After three highly successful years Jimi Hendrix, Mitch Mitchell and Noel Redding it seemed had decided to go their own ways last year. Noel Redding formed Fat Mattress which appears to have unformed itself already and Mitch has joined Jack Bruce's outfit as one of his "Friends".

EXPERIENCE

"The thing about the Experience was that it was a trio," Jimi informed me on a visit to London. "There were only so many things we could do as a trio but when we find some more things to do there's no reason why we can't get together again."

Jimi has already played a few gigs in America with his new unit, "The Band of Gipsies" but Mitch Mitchell has flown over on two occasions to join Jimi and now they are all talking of a re-union tour for the Experience.

'TEENYBOPPER'

On the "teenybopper" scene things have really been falling apart and in quick succession Andy Fairweather Low announced his "abdication" from Amen Corner, Steve Ellis left the Love Affair and Dave Dee left Dozy, Beaky, Mick and Tich.

DAVE DEE

Dave told the Press that he was quitting after nine years with the group because their winning run of hit singles seemed to have finished and he wanted to explore the possibilities of an acting career. Steve Ellis left the Love Affair because, like Frampton and Marriott he was tired of being screamed at.

STEVE ELLIS

"I used to go on stage knock myself out shouting for three quarters of an hour and come off sweating like a pig," said Steve. "I just want a chance after three years to prove that I can sing and to get people to listen."

ANDY FAIRWEATHER LOW

Andy Fairweather Low was another reluctant idol but more important he claimed to have become a vocalist by accident!

AMEN CORNER

"I formed Amen Corner as a soul band originally drawn from the best musicians in and around Cardiff," said Andy. "I intended to be a guitarist but we found outselves with too many guitars and no vocalist. I liked the sound the band had and rather than break up the pattern I agreed to fill in on vocals for a time. Suddenly I found I had created my own monster—a kind of 'Andy Pandy' creature who was bigger than our music. Nothing is more important to me than the music—that's why I got out."

THE HOLLIES

Another group which lost a key member last year were the Hollies who parted company with Graham Nash whom they lost to Crosby, Stills and Nash. At the time the split was hardly amicable as Graham's more idealistic musical ambition conflicted with the other Hollies' simple philosophy that to be good entertainers was enough.

Says vocalist Allan Clarke, "Naturally we worried at first because Graham had taken a large part in our early success but we've proved we can still make it on our own and with Terry Sylvester taking part on our two big hits since the split, (*Sorry Suzanne* and *He Ain't Heavy*) we have a new confidence."

Since the break-up Graham has been back to Britain for a highly successful concert with Dave Crosby and Steve Stills at the Royal Albert Hall and the early antagonism has been healed. Graham stayed some while with Hollie Tony Hicks in London before leaving again for America.

THE BEE GEES

The Bee Gees were another ensemble who begged to differ last year and following guitarist Vince Melouney went drummer Colin Petersen ("Did he leave or was he pushed?") followed by Robin Gibb making it quite clear

there was a difference of opinion between himself and Barry, Maurice Gibb married Lulu and did a touch of the "Yes I've left, no I haven'ts" giving us all the distinct impression that shortly we shall hear that ominous announcement— "Ladies and Gentlemen – the Bee Gee!"

SIXTIES

The most saddening split to me personally was one which did not receive the dramatic coverage afforded some of our other groups. It was the dispersement of the Bonzo Dogs who were, for any who loved and listened, the pop conscience of the Sixties. They debunked and denuded so much of the pretention and pomposity of pop. No one was safe from the satirical snipe of the Bonzo's.

They were a great deal better musically than anyone ever gave them credit for but Viv Stanshall and Legs Larry Smith are still marching on so we live in hope of their solo swipes.

CONCLUSION

The conclusion to all the recent coming and going of pop units would seem to illustrate one thing more clearly than anything else – in pop nothing is certain and the marriage of three or more personalities in one unit is no easy thing.

PETER MARINELLO

Name: Peter Marinello.

Born: Edinburgh, Scotland.

Age: 20.

Height: 5 ft. 8 in.

Weight: 10 st. 2 lb.

Occupation: Footballer, super-winger for Arsenal, knocking on door for Scottish representative honours.

Value in transfer market: £100,000 paid for him by Arsenal to Hibernian.

Playing style: Daring and determined, fantastic ball-control, capable of scoring goals but adept at creating them. So fast that few opponents can tackle him.

Personal characteristics: Slightly built, narrow-shouldered, flowing, long, dark brown hair, shy-smiling which matches his introvert off-duty personality.

Business interests: Newspaper columnist, but much in demand by agents to start modelling, acting, even pop-singing.

Pop music likes: Hard-swinging music, particularly in the underground style. Specially rates Spooky Tooth, Chicago, Georgie Fame.

Marital status: Engaged to Scots girl Joyce Murray, a childhood sweetheart who joined him in London soon after he signed for Arsenal.

Temperament: Fairly even and quiet off the field, but with sudden flashes of fury during a game. He's let his fist fly once or twice, but more as a threat than an actual punch-up. As a player he likes to be in the thick of the action and his beautifully controlled style sometimes leads him to make opponents look a bit stupid. This leads to retaliation but Marinello is slowly learning to curb his outbursts of temper.

Taste in girls: Has no fixed ideas about colour of hair but likes small, slim girls who don't try to show off and are prepared to accept Peter as a person not a celebrity.

Taste in clothes: Flamboyant. Loves Donegal Tweed suits, massive kipper ties, maxi-raincoats . . . an essentially modern taste but he does not like ultra-violent colours. Admits to spending "rather too much" on clothes but believes that a footballer at top level should dress well as does a star actor or singer.

Worst moment: At the age of eighteen, seriously thinking of giving up football. He had had one season as a "wonder boy" discovery, then lost form and was dropped by the Hibernian manager, Bob Shankly. Marinello was out for a month, convinced he just didn't have the right temperament but accepted the manager's advice: "If you play badly, don't mope—just work harder to sort things out."

Favourite food: Massive steaks, Dover sole with the trimmings. Perhaps a glass of beer.

Home life: Digs, selected for him by Arsenal's management. Would like one day to invest in a home of his own, but not until after he gets married. Does not enjoy late nights and sleeps soundly.

Name: George Best.

Born: Belfast, Northern Ireland.

Age: 24.

Height: 5 ft. 8½ in.

Weight: 10 st. 3 lb.

Occupation: Footballer, super-winger for Manchester United and Northern Ireland. Voted Footballer of the Year and European Player of the Year before his 23rd birthday.

Value in transfer market: At least £250,000.

Playing style: Fast and tricky, incredible ball-control, world class taker and maker of goals. Feared and often fouled by opposing defenders.

Personal characteristics: Flowing dark-brown, nearly black, hair—was known as "El Beatle" by Continental fans. Flashing white smile. Piercing blue eyes.

Business interests: Ownership of boutiques, TV and newspaper advertising, sponsorship of sports goods.

Pop music likes: Most current top ten records; Lulu; Tom Jones; Hollies.

Marital status: Unattached but was engaged, briefly, to blonde Danish model Eva Haraldstat.

Temperament: Off-duty, hard to rile, but he shows anger when unknown people try to muscle in on his privacy. On the pitch, sometimes criticised for his flashes of anger and his petulant displays against referees. Was sent off once—in a World Club Championship game and was suspended for four weeks for knocking the ball out of the ref's hands. Overall, though, he has shown remarkable restraint considering how closely marked he is.

Taste in girls: Long hair, preferably blonde—but says he notices a girl's legs first. Hates the "sham" who tags along just because he is a personality. Likes a girl who can talk on subjects other than soccer.

Taste in clothes: Buys slacks and sweaters by the dozen and prefers casual gear to formal suits. Wears one pair of boots or shoes until they are worn out, then buys a new pair. At one time designed menswear for his boutique but now can't find ideas. Prefers the mini look for girls. Providing the legs are the right shape!

Worst moment: Arriving at Old Trafford, Manchester, at the age of 15 and feeling so homesick that he went back home to Ireland. This could have wrecked his career before it started, but manager Matt Busby was patient enough to invite the skinny youngster back for a fresh start.

Favourite food: Steak, scampi, Spanish dishes, washed down by the occasional lager or glass of wine. Would one day like to open his own restaurant in the Manchester area.

Home life: Until recently, lived with landlady Mrs. Fullaway in digs, but bought a £30,000 house in Cheshire, complete with swimming pool and sports room. It's already a Mecca for sight-seers.

TOMORROW

EDISON LIGHTHOUSE by Peter Pugh-Cook

LULU

Lulu was born Marie McDonald McLaughlin Lawrie on November 3rd, 1948 in Lennox Castle, Lennoxton. She is 5 ft. 2in. tall, weighs 7 st. 4 lb. and has green eyes and red hair. She started singing at the age of three.

CLIFF RICHARD

Cliff was born Harry Roger Webb, on October 14th, 1940 in Lucknow, India. (He came to England in 1947.) He stands 5 ft. 11 in. tall and weighs 10 st., he has dark brown hair and eyes. Cliff sat for his G.C.E. O-level in Religious Instruction (1967) and passed. He has written two books.

CANNED HEAT

Bob "The Bear" Hite – Vocalist and occasional harmonica. He was born in 1944 and weighs twenty stone.

Al "Blind Owl" Wilson – Slide and rhythm guitar, harmonica and vocals. He was also born in 1944. He writes many of Canned Heat's songs.

Larry "The Mole" Taylor – Bass guitar. At fourteen he started playing professional bass with Jerry Lee Lewis

and he's worked on more sessions than anyone else in the group.

Adolfo "Fito" De La Parra – Drummer. Spent most of his early playing in Mexico. He has played with a few of the biggest Mexican groups

Harvey "The Snake" Mande – Lead guitar. Born in Detroit in 1946 and moved to Chicago as a youngster. He bought his first guitar at the age of sixteen.

TREMELOES

Alan Blakely was born on April 1st, 1942 in Bromley, Kent. He is 5 ft. 9 in. tall. Alan married Linda Stevens on November 30th, 1969.

Leonard "Chip" Hawkes was born on November 2nd, 1945 in Shepherds Bush, London. He is 5 ft. 9 in. tall and has brown eyes and hair. He married Carol Dilworth on October 19th, 1969.

Dave Munden was born on December 2nd, 1943 in Dagenham, Essex. He is 6 ft. tall, and has brown hair and eyes. Dave is married to Bunny girl Andree Wittenberg.

Rick West was born on May 7th, 1943 in Dagenham, Essex. He is 5 ft. 11 in. tall and has blue eyes and dark brown hair. Rick married Linda in August, 1963.

TINY TIM

Tiny Tim first began singing under his present name in the fifties in Greenwich Village. But it wasn't until he became a regular performer in a mid-town nightspot that his talent was finally recognised. Since then he has achieved tremendous popularity, appearing on television shows over here as well as in America. He was married in 1969.

DUSTY SPRINGFIELD

Dusty was born on April 16th, 1940 in Hampstead, London. She has green eyes and blonde hair, stands 5 ft. 3½ in. and weighs 8 st. 1 lb. She says the turning point in her career was when she joined The Springfields in 1960. Dusty dislikes garlic, cold weather and early rising.

BEACH BOYS

Dennis Wilson born on December 4th, 1944, in Hawthorne, California. He has brown hair, blue eyes, stands 5 ft. 9 in., and weighs 11 st. 8 lb. Dennis is the group's glad-hander, good-timer and mad-mixer.

Carl Wilson born on December 21st, 1946, in Hawthorne, California. He has dark brown hair, blue eyes, stands 5 ft. 10 in. and weighs 12 st. 7 lb.

Mike Love was born on March 15th, 1941, in Los Angeles. He has blond hair, blue eyes, and is 6 ft. 1 in. tall, and weighs 11 st. 13 lb.

Alan Jardine was born on September 3rd, 1942, in Lima, Ohio. He has blond hair, blue eyes, is 5 ft. 5 in. and weighs 9 st. 2 lb.

Bruce Johnston was born on June 27th, 1944 in Chicago. He has brown hair, blue eyes, stands 5 ft. 8 in. and weighs 10 st. 9 lb. Bruce joined the group as Beach Boy number six in 1965.

NICE

Brian Davidson was born on May 25th, 1942 in Leicester. He is 5 ft. 7 in. tall, weighs 10 st. and has brown hair and eyes. Brian is married to Maureen.

Lee Jackson was born on January 8th, 1943 in Newcastle upon Tyne. He is 5 ft. 11 in. tall, weighs 10 st. 8 lb. and has brown hair and grey/green eyes.

Keith Emerson was born on November 2nd, 1944 in Todmorden, Lancs. He is 5 ft. 9 in. tall, weighs 9 st. 5 lb. and has blue eyes and brown hair.

SANDIE SHAW

Sandie Shaw was born Sandra Ann Goodrich on February 26th, 1947, in Dagenham, Essex. She is 5 ft. 8 in. tall, has blue eyes and dark brown hair. Her biggest break came when Adam Faith discovered her. She is married to Fashion Designer Jeff Banks.

ELVIS

"The King" was born on January 8th, 1935, in Toleo, Mississippi. He stands 6 ft. tall and weighs 11½ st. and has blue/grey eyes and black hair. He likes boxing and touch football. He has been making hits since 1957 and has also made many films.

THE WHO

Keith Moon – Drummer. Born August 23rd, 1946, in Wembley. Has black hair, brown eyes and is 5 ft. 9 in. tall. He was educated at a school in Harrow and entered show-biz at the age of sixteen.

Roger Daltry – Lead singer. Born March 1st, 1945 in Hammersmith. He is 5 ft. 7 in. tall with blue eyes, and, according to him, assorted hair! His hobby is fishing.

Pete Townsend – Lead guitar. Born May 19th, 1945 in Chiswick. He stands 6 ft. tall, has blue eyes and brown/black hair. He likes The Beatles, Stockhausen, Bach and The Stones.

John Entwhistle – Bass guitar. Born October 9th, 1945 in Chiswick. He is 5 ft. 11½ in. tall and has blue eyes. John can play bass guitar, trumpet, french horn.

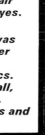

JACK WILD by Roger Brown

BADFINGER

Pete Ham was born on April 27th, 1947, and he started the group called The Iveys. He played harmonica at the age of four, and when he was twelve he started the guitar. He says, "I think we conned our way into Apple (their recording company) at first. We didn't deserve it; we weren't that good."

Mike Gibbons was born on March 12th, 1949, has red hair and freckles, and was once described as having the smile of a kid caught pinching the bread and jam. Mike learned to play the drums when he joined his first military band.

Joe Molland was born on June 21st, 1947. He was the last to join Badfinger. He left school at the age of fifteen, and started his working life as a messenger boy with a Liverpool shipping office.

Tom Evans was born on June 5th, 1947. He says that he is in the music business for good. "I couldn't get out of it now." He started in Liverpool with the Calderstones, the local teen bopper group, one of the local idols.

JOE COCKER

Joe Robert Cocker was born on May 20th, 1944 in Sheffield. He attended the Central Technical School and later went on to become a gas fitter. Joe is 5 ft. 9 in. tall, weighs 11 st. 10 lb. and has brown hair and blue/green eyes. He said that he spends most of his money enjoying himself and we all agree that that is the best way to spend it!

CILLA BLACK

Cilla was born Priscilla Maria Veronica White, in Liverpool on May 27th, 1943. She has red hair and dark blue eyes, and stands 5 ft. 5 in. tall. Her first film comedy Work . . . Is A Four-Letter Word, was filmed at Pinewood. She said after her last day there: "It's dead easy — a big tea break. A piece of cake."

JIMMY CLIFF

Jimmy was born on July 30th, 1947 in Jamaica. He is 5 ft. 8 in. tall, weighs 9 st. 7 lb. and has brown eyes and dark brown hair. His first big hit was Wonderful World, Beautiful People. Jimmy made the record in his native Jamaica but later he recorded it in New York.

Donovan first appeared on your television screen in January 1965, in the programme Ready, Steady, Go. His real name is Donovan Phillip Leitch and he was born on May 10th, 1946. He is 5 ft. 8 in. tall and has green eyes and black hair. Donovan's discs include Catch The Wind, which was his first record and hit, Colours, Mellow Yellow and Sunshine Superman.

DONOVAN

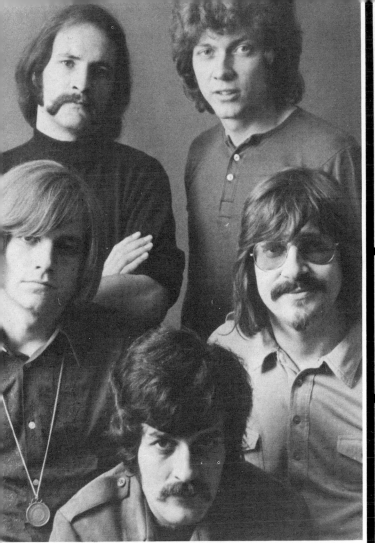

MARY HOPKIN

Mary Hopkin was born on May 3rd, 1950 in Pontardawe, Wales. She is 5 ft. 5 in. tall, weighs 7 st. 13 lb. and has blonde hair and blue eyes. Mary's talent was first spotted by Twiggy when she appeared on Opportunity Knocks and Twiggy in turn mentioned her to Paul McCartney. Since then she has risen to greater and greater heights.

BOBBIE GENTRY

Bobbie Gentry is twenty-three years old and comes from Chickasaw County, Mississippi. She has dark hair and brown eyes and first became a performer when she was eleven. Since then she has composed several dozen songs and learnt to play the piano, banjo, vibes and electric bass.

HOLLIES

The five original members of The Hollies were Allan Clarke, Don Rathbone, Eric Haydock, Graham Nash and Tony Hicks. When Don left the group in 1963 he was replaced on drums by Bobby Elliot. Later, in mid 1966, Eric left and Bern Calvert took over on bass guitar. Lastly, in 1968 Graham left and his place was taken by Terry Sylvester.

Allan Clarke was born on April 5th, 1942, in Salford, Lancs. He is 5 ft. 10½ in. tall, weighs 10 st. 7 lb. and has black hair and brown eyes.

Tony Hicks was born in Nelson, Lancs on December 16th, 1945. He is 5 ft. 11 in. tall, weighs 10 st. and has blue eyes and brown hair.

Bobby Elliot was born on December 8th, 1942 in Burnley, Lancs. He is 6 ft. tall, weighs 10 st. 10 lb. and has fair hair and grey eyes.

Bernard Calvert was born in Burnley, on September 16th, 1942. He is 5 ft. 10 in. tall, weighs 10 st. 7 lb. and has brown hair and eyes.

Terry Sylvester was born on January 8th, 1947 in Liverpool. He is 5 ft. 11 in. tall, weighs 10 st. 5 lb. and has black hair and brown eyes.

MOODY BLUES

The former members of this group were Denny Laine, Graeme Edge, Clint Warwick, Mike Pinder and Ray Thomas. But now there have been two changes; Denny Laine and Clint Warwick have left and Justin Hayward and John Lodge have taken over in their place. The Moody Blues launched their own record company in 1969. It is called "Threshold" and they concentrate mainly on LPs.

SUE GEORGE by Roger Morton

CLIFF RICHARD by Dezo Hoffman

LOU CHRISTIE

Lou Christie's real name is Lugee Geno Sacco and he was born in Glen Willard, Pennsylvania. He soared to fame with such records as The Gipsy Cried and Lightning Strikes, which were both million sellers. Lou is loved by fans everywhere and his disc I'm Gonna Make You Mine was yet another smash hit for him.

STEVIE WONDER

Stevie Wonder was born in Saginaw, Michigan and was the third child in a family of six. Although Stevie was blind at birth he has overcome his disability and is now brilliant at playing drums, organ, piano and harmonica. Some of his more popular records include High Heel Sneakers, Harmonica Man, Fingertips, Water Boy, Yesterme Yesteryou Yesterday.

EDISON LIGHTHOUSE

Ray Dorey — Vocalist. Born February 22nd, 1949, in Windsor. He is 6 ft. 1½ in. (the tallest in the group), weighs 11 st. 7 lb. and has blond hair and blue eyes.

Dave Taylor — Bass guitar and vocals. Was born on October 7th, 1950, in Windsor. He stands 5 ft. 8 in. tall, weighs 9 st. 8 lb. and has black hair and brown eyes.

Stuart Edwards — Lead guitar and vocals. Born on June 9th, 1946, in Windsor. He is 5 ft. 11 in. tall with black hair and brown eyes.

George Weyman — Drums. Was born on April 18th, 1949, in Windsor. He is 5 ft. 9 in. tall, weighs 10 st. 3 lb., and has green eyes and brown hair.

D. B. M. & T.

Dozy was born Trevor Davies on November 27th, 1944. He is 5 ft. 11 in. tall, has brown eyes and brown hair and weighs 10 st. 7 lb. Dozy plays bass guitar and does his share of singing since Dave Dee left.

Beaky was born John Dymond on July 10th, 1944. He is 5 ft. 11 in. tall with brown hair and blue eyes, and weighs 10 st. Beaky is on rhythm guitar and also sings.

Tich was born Ian Amey on May 15th, 1944. He is 5 ft. 8 in. (the smallest in the group), has blond hair and brown eyes and weighs 10 st. He is on lead guitar and sings as well.

Mick was born Michael Wilson on March 4th, 1944. He is 6 ft. tall with brown hair and green eyes and weighs 12 st. Mick is on the drums, and is the only one who does not sing, because he says he can't.

LOVE AFFAIR

The Love Affair were formed in answer to advertisements in the musical press, put in by Sidney Bacon, father of Mo Bacon, the group's drummer. Other members of the group are Rex Brayley, the lead guitarist, Morgan Fisher, the organist, Mick Jackson, bass guitar, and Auguste Eadon, who took over from Steve Ellis, lead singer, who left to go solo.

HUMBLE PIE

Steve Marriott was born on January 30th, 1947 in Bow, London. He is 5 ft. 5 in. tall, weighs 8 st. and has green eyes and brown hair. Steve was originally with The Small Faces and his likes include peace and quiet.

Peter Frampton, also from another famous group The Herd, was born on April 22nd, 1950, in Beckenham. He is 5 ft. 8 in. tall, weighs 7 st. 8 lb. and has bluish eyes and brown hair.

Greg Ridley was born on October 23rd, 1947 in Aspatria. He is 5 ft. 11 in. tall, weighs 9½ st. and has blue eyes and blackish hair. Greg likes the music of Jack Bruce and he dislikes shaving.

Jerry Shirley is the youngest member of Humble Pie and he was born on February 4th, 1952, in Waltham Cross. He is 5 ft. 5 in. tall, weighs 8½ st. and has blue eyes and dark brown hair. Watch out for Jerry if you are ever in Ibiza, because that is his favourite place!

CLODAGH ROGERS

Clodagh Rogers was born in Co. Down on March 5th, 1947. She is 5 ft. 3½ in. tall, weighs 7 st. 7 lb. and has blonde hair and green eyes. Clodagh is married to records promotion manager John Morris and her likes include sunbathing, money and clothes.

FLEETWOOD MAC

Peter Green was born on October 29th 1946. He stands 5 ft. 8 in., weighs 9 st. 7 lb., and has brown eyes and brown hair. He has two brothers and a sister. Pete can play the guitar and harmonica and his hobbies are : collecting old records, antique guns, knives etc.

Danny Kirwan was born on May 13th 1950. He is 5 ft. 10 in. tall, weighs 9 st. 12 lb. and has green eyes and fair hair. He dislikes lack of common sense but likes unattached women. His best friend is Peter Green.

John McVie was born on November 26th 1945. He is 5 ft. 9 in. tall, has green eyes and brown hair and weighs 10 st. 7 lb. John is married to Christine Perfect who used to be with the group Chicken Shack. His favourite actress is Kim Novak.

Mick Fleetwood was born on June 24th, 1947. He is a giant at 6 ft. 6 in. weighs 10 st. 4 lb. with hazel eyes and fair hair. He dislikes pomposity and deceit, and likes de luxe sports cars and antique furniture

Jeremy Spencer was born on July 4th, 1948. He is the smallest of the group at 5 ft. 4 in.; he weighs 7 st. 7 lb. and has green eyes and dark brown hair. His wife's name is Fiona, and they have a son Dicken. Jeremy can play the guitar and piano.

GEORGIE FAME

Real name Clive Powell. Georgie was born on June 26th, 1943 in Leigh, Lancashire. He is 5 ft. 8 in. tall with brown hair and blue eyes. Five and a half years ago Georgie had his first number one record called Yeh Yeh.

DAVE DEE

Dave Dee was born David Harman on December 17th, 1943. He was originally a policeman but left because he was too kind hearted and couldn't arrest people. He then joined with Dozy, Beaky, Mick and Tich, making such hit records as Hold Tight, Hideaway, Okay and Legend of Xanadu. Dave is 6 ft. tall, weighs 11 st. 12 lb. and has light brown hair and blue eyes.

29

MICK JAGGER by courtesy of United Artists

PAUL NEWMAN by David Sutton

You can make it if you try

If you can't afford to buy all the lovely clothes in the shops the only answer (which wouldn't get you arrested!) is to make them yourself. Now don't faint dead away 'cos sewing isn't nearly so difficult once you get goin'. The thought is worse than the action! To launch you on this new cut-it-out campaign, we've chosen some super but simple-to-make styles. Some you can send to us for diagram details and instructions and some we have chosen are by Simplicity and Style, the pattern people.

Spring **is when a young bird's fancy turns to thoughts of "Blimey I've got nothing to wear, where's the money coming from anyway and what's in?!!" What's in, can of course, change from one month to the next. Your favourite fashion editor may be rabbitting on about gypsies and peasants but that doesn't mean every single bird in Britain is wearing nothing but hoop earrings and patchwork every day of her life does it? Some things are never out, like the three numbers we've illustrated here.**

Yours truly can't remember one single year (and I'm going back to B.C.!) when shirt dresses weren't all the rage! It's the material you make this dress in that makes it "in". A pretty print is always great, you can make it plain with white collar and cuffs, in cotton voile or light-weight wool, in mini, midi or maxi. And you can make one for him too. (Which should put the spring into his step!) Send to us for the how-to-do-it.

I can't see smocking dying the death for quite a long time so a sweet little dress like this one would come in handy for spring things. Plain or printed this dress would be pretty but I'd steer clear of anything too heavily patterned. This style needs a light touch. It is a Style Pattern No. 2742. (If you have any difficulty getting it, that address too, is on page 35.)

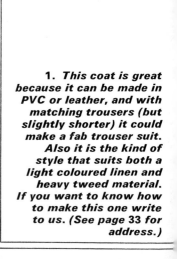

1. This coat is great because it can be made in PVC or leather, and with matching trousers (but slightly shorter) it could make a fab trouser suit. Also it is the kind of style that suits both a light coloured linen and heavy tweed material. If you want to know how to make this one write to us. (See page 33 for address.)

Spring

drawings by TINA FAVEL

a) Towelling bandeaus are unbelievably useful and dead easy to make. You can make one to suit all your swimsuits and look really stunning without spending too much.
b) Why not make your towel better than everybody else's by adding some super fringes? What could be easier? White fringes on any colour look great but try your own combination of colours to make an effect that will have the life guards running—in your direction!
c) A summer without a bikini is like a skiing holiday with no snow. Useless! This one (Style Pattern 2759) has a super shaped top and nice shorts-shaped pants which look really great in navy towelling with white trim, or stretch towelling or Helanca, or even plain cotton. Plain or stripes look best, it's a bit too sporty for flowers unless you use a Hawaiian print and then . . . it's a style with man appeal!

If you have a million dates to look forward to (or even if you're just hopeful) you need something extra special and cool to wear like this tiny top and trousers outfit. You can make it with or without sleeves and a great idea would be to make the sleeves see-through and the legs see-through too but line the body bits! (If it does turn out to be a cool summer that should make the temperature soar!) (Write to us.)

For any of the styles I've mentioned you can get from US, write to: FAB ANNUAL

FASHION, Fabulous-208, Fleetway House, Farringdon Street, London, E.C.4. (Please enclose an s.a.e.)

If you can't get any of the Style or Simplicity Patterns mentioned, you can enquire about them by writing to: Metropolis House, 39–45, Tottenham Court Road, London W.1.

Summer's a terrible time 'cos you want so much stuff and you know in your heart of hearts there's only going to be two sunny days! (But if you're one of the enormous band of optimists you'll really believe it's going to be tropical and get prepared accordingly!) As we belong to that band we've got these super suggestions for making your summer swing.

Summer
by HEATHER KIRBY

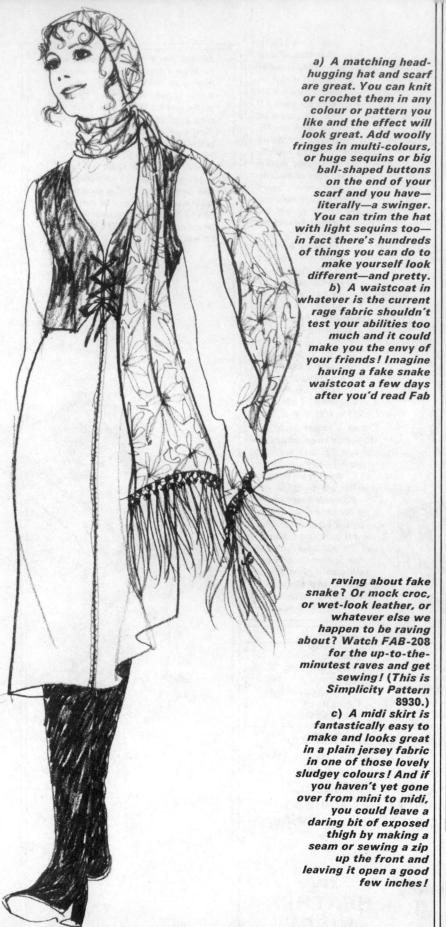

a) A matching head-hugging hat and scarf are great. You can knit or crochet them in any colour or pattern you like and the effect will look great. Add woolly fringes in multi-colours, or huge sequins or big ball-shaped buttons on the end of your scarf and you have—literally—a swinger. You can trim the hat with light sequins too—in fact there's hundreds of things you can do to make yourself look different—and pretty.

b) A waistcoat in whatever is the current rage fabric shouldn't test your abilities too much and it could make you the envy of your friends! Imagine having a fake snake waistcoat a few days after you'd read Fab

raving about fake snake? Or mock croc, or wet-look leather, or whatever else we happen to be raving about? Watch FAB-208 for the up-to-the-minutest raves and get sewing! (This is Simplicity Pattern 8930.)

c) A midi skirt is fantastically easy to make and looks great in a plain jersey fabric in one of those lovely sludgey colours! And if you haven't yet gone over from mini to midi, you could leave a daring bit of exposed thigh by making a seam or sewing a zip up the front and leaving it open a good few inches!

Autumn is a time of mellow fruitfulness and all that jazz. Also it can bring you down after the lovely long summer days. But the scene is to be positive about things and if you try you can make autumn the most happening season of them all. (A word of extra comfort for plumpies: you can start hiding arms, legs etc. again!!)

We'd love to make one of these floppy hats but it looks a bit difficult! So instead it's probably a better idea to, a) buy one in the summer sales, b) get the money off your Ma, or c) hunt around in the local jumble sales because they must have thousands. Then doll it up to suit yourself with a piece of petersham, a belt or a scarf.

Autumn

Winter is full of cold dark nights—just right for staying at home and getting on with some sewing! But you don't have to make dreary gearies! Why not make yourself a maxi for this winter? Or a safari jacket (and if you're really clever, one for him too?)

You can make almost any long jacket into a safari jacket just by adding four pockets and a belt with a buckle. But if you want to make the real McCoy and start from scratch, write to us.

Ever thought of making a pair of jeans? Are we joking? Why not? They aren't nearly as hard as trousers. So long as you use tougher'n tough fabric and fit them on yourself nice 'n tight they should be O.K. Also if you don't fancy the thought of all that work you can make quite an ordinary pair of pants look jean-like just by adding a few pockets with the rows of double stitching round them and also the tabs for a belt in all the right places. (Tip: when you're making the tabs, decide which belt you're most likely to wear and make them the right width—or you'll be sorry. 'Cos you'll find the belt is wider than the tabs!)

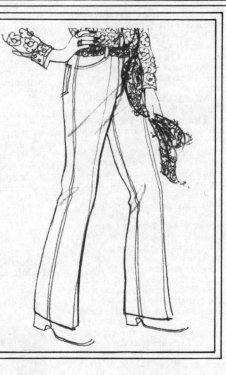

This maxi is both stunning and simple. The huge collar can keep out the snow drifts (!) and the very simple shape could be reversed. So you'd have two coats instead of one! (This is a Style Pattern 2891.)

Winter

I REMEMBER at the time I was biting the end of my gloved thumb and wondering if I could be had up for what I was doing.

Did it count as false pretences? Or fraud?

"It couldn't be as bad as that," I thought to myself. "After all I'm not costing anybody anything. Am I?"

The door on the far side of the counter opened softly—the door marked F. Cornelius Carruthers, F.R.S.A., F.V.I. and F.V.A. A head looked out and scanned me. I pretended not to notice. It was a time for showing my cool. If I went on like this there would be a hole right through the thumb of my glove. I put my hand on my lap hastily.

The head withdrew, but the door stayed open. So I looked. On the inside wall I could see one of those office pep notices TIME IS MONEY.

So I was costing somebody something. If time was money I was wasting somebody's time—quite a lot of it. What, did someone who was an F.R.S.A. and F.V.I. as well as an F.V.A. get paid by the hour? By the hour? That was ridiculous. He couldn't be an old scrubber on piece-work, not Mr. Cornelius Carruthers.

Mr. Cornelius Carruthers sounded quite petrifying.

The door opened and a young man came out. It wasn't the owner of the head that had just looked at me round the same door. It was a younger head and nicer.

"Miss Blakey?" he asked. "Miss Holly Blakey?"

"That's right!" I stifled a desire to put my thumb back in my mouth.

"So you want permission to view the property?" he said. "Ashcombe House in Fiddler's Lane?"

"Please!"

"A very desirable property indeed," he said, looking me over in a way I wasn't sure I liked. Or disliked either. "Our asking price is thirteen thousand."

So he expected me to drop dead at the mention of that? "I know," I assured him, as if thirteen thousand was what I carried around in small change. I reckoned if he knew I was a junior member of the typing pool at Egham Investments (Overseas) Ltd., he would probably drop dead himself. Certainly he would curl his handsome lip.

"Perhaps I should warn you," he said in his rather superior, cut-glass manner, "that we are already negotiating for this property. We may well conclude the sale this afternoon."

It was my chance to cut and run for it. I knew I could

He was impressed. I was glad I had decided to wear my new scarlet trousers and the short embroidered caftan. What with that and the casual, floating chiffon scarf, maybe I had fooled him.

never buy a thirteen thousand pound house, not in a million years. The trouble with me is that when I'm scared I get cheeky.

"I'd better hurry up and see it then," I said.

He was impressed. I was glad I had decided to wear my brand new scarlet trousers and the short embroidered caftan. What with that and the casual, floating chiffon scarf maybe I had fooled him.

"Indeed we had," he said. "I'll take you out there myself, straight away."

"Y-you don't have to do that!" Panic-stricken I was remembering time was money in this estate agent's office. And from my shining new hair do down to my glossy new M & S patent shoes, I was a dead waste of time in anybody's language.

"But please," he said, "we like to look after our important customers. Please step this way."

IT GOT worse!

AROUND the back of the offices was a shining, sleek sports car. I don't know much about cars but this was one of those that seemed all engine and room for the seats had been added on as an afterthought.

The young man helped me in with a flourish. He had longish fair hair and dead cheeky eyes. His grin was all nice and quirky, and if I hadn't had butterflies where the lunch I hadn't eaten should have been I'd have gone overboard for him.

He started the car quietly enough. He almost tiptoed it

out of the parking yard. Then he put his foot down and we went off like an Apollo moonshot. I lost my breath straight away.

It took us seven minutes flat to get to Fiddler's Lane and it would have taken me fifty-five minutes by bus.

"Not bad, huh?" he asked me proudly, patting the car as if it were a favourite Borzoi hound.

"If time is money," I said, "it must save you an awful lot of money!"

"What?" He laughed. "Oh, that notice in the old man's office. I see what you mean. Well, that's Ashcombe House! Let's go in."

"Would you mind," I asked him, "if I went in by myself. Alone? Please!"

"What?"

"I'd really prefer it."

"I won't give you the old sales talk," he said. "If that's what you're bothered about."

"I'd sooner be alone."

It was quite odd the way he sagged. From being a bright, chirpy, assured young man he suddenly looked vulnerable and fed up. The wind had dropped and his sails were drooping.

"But of course," he said, "I'll open the door for you."

I DIDN'T mean to stay long. It was just shocking curiosity that had taken me there anyway. I walked through the huge open plan lounge and admired the deep set fireplace with the inglenook seats. The kitchen was a "Formica" heaven with built in dream cupboards. The decor was expensive and fresh and new.

Three bedrooms, one so big

you could practically play badminton in it, if that was what you wanted to do.

"Good old Billy," I thought. "Billy, you've got it made. Just what you always wanted."

Billy Marvin! Now William J. Marvin! Now the prospective bridegroom of Daphne Heron, daughter of an alderman and some company chairman somewhere. This gorgeous house was the father's present to the bride and groom. Oh, yes, William J. Marvin had got it made all right.

When he had been Billy Marvin he'd been my boy friend. We'd pedalled our bikes together and eaten chips out of the same newspaper. Now he'd moved on and got himself into a different bracket.

I smiled to myself. It wasn't a broken heart situation. I'd just been a kid then. Love hadn't really come into it. It was just plain, gawping curiosity that had brought me here to bluff my way into the house that would one day be Billy's home.

I looked out of the window and saw the young man waiting in the garden. He was the sort of young man who went with a house like this.

Smooth. Streamlined, with bags of assurance. He would know what to do anywhere and anytime. He had polish as well. He was probably the son of the boss, driving that dishy sports car. He'd probably spend his evenings in night clubs, dancing cheek to cheek with smoochy heiresses.

Well, goodbye Billy. Goodbye to this sort of thing. This was how the other half lived and the other half would definitely stay

Shaming The Devil

By Derek Long

the other half as far as I was concerned.

I was just Holly, a typist with a bit of cheek and no illusions about herself.

Pity really. He was a nice young man, too. I could have gone for him, but I knew I'd die of shame now to admit I was a minnow in the typing pool and if he took me in one of his posh places I'd probably not know the difference between a Campari and a dry sherry.

I saw the young man start. Then in the most extraordinary way he slunk up to the hedge and crept along to the house. The last five yards was almost one leap and he was inside. I could hear him calling from below.

"Hey, where are you, Miss Blakey. Quick!"

"Would you mind," I asked him, "if I went in by myself? Alone? Please!" "But of course," he said. "I'll open the door for you."

We met on the stairs in collision. He grabbed me and steadied me.

"What's up?"

"Please," he said. "Would you mind if we got out of here? A bit sharpish like."

"But why?"

"The house isn't really for sale," he said feverishly. "And the client who is buying is here. With the boss. In a Rolls Royce."

"You mean Mr. Marvin?"

"Himself," he said, "with his fiancée and her father. And Mr. Carruthers as well."

Billy was here! I felt my cheeks begin to burn. Fancy being seen here, me, just gawping round the house that would one day be his.

"What're we waiting for?" I said frantically. "Come on then!"

"The back way," he said. "Cor, that's great of you."

THE BACK way out had snags. Like a locked door in a garden fence. The young man practically had to lift me up and throw me over. I could feel my tights ladder all the way up. He tried to vault it after me and fell on his back.

"The car," he said. "Come on."

We tore up a little lane hand in hand and there was no ceremonious door opening this time. We shot off like a shell out of a tank gun and headed back for the office.

"Slow down, slow down," I yelled at him. "Just tell me what this is all about."

He pulled the car into a lay-by and stopped. He drew out a tatty packet of cigarettes and offered me one. Not that I smoke. He started to laugh.

"That's me all over," he said. "I might have guessed this would happen."

"What?"

"Shouldn't be using this car," he said. "It belongs to the boss's son."

"You mean—you *pinched* it?"

"Not quite," he said. "I'm just the office dogsbody. Young Mr. Carruthers junior is playing golf this afternoon. So as usual I have the keys of his flaming car. 'Fill the car with petrol, boy. Get it serviced. Then bring it round to me at the club, there's a good fellow.'"

"But not," I said, "to use it for driving clients round to view houses. Why did you do it?"

He started to grin. It was a nice grin and I took to it.

"I've a car as well," he said. "A beat up old jalopy. I call it Snoopy. I like Snoopy. But you can't pull smashing birds in Snoopy."

"You mean—"

(*Continued on page 75*)

"Heartbroken, Luton"

Now I've always considered myself a pretty ordinary sort of bloke. I was keener on sport than spelling at school. Interested in girls just as soon as I realised they weren't the same as boys. Happy with a career in the police force until I found out I could sing a bit . . . so I ended up in show business.

Forget the title "pop star"—I hate it. You get lucky, make a few hits but that doesn't make you a star. It just makes you lucky, that's all.

Nobody ever heard of the police cadet named David Harman. But the name Dave Dee got around a bit. And suddenly I was being interviewed about all sorts of things . . . fashion, politics, religion, sex. At first, I felt a bit daft. After all, what bloke hasn't looked at those cosy women's magazine features full of advice to the lovelorn; and what bloke hasn't sniggered at the answers to letters signed "Heartbroken, Luton"

Then the editor of FAB-208 got on the phone. "Dave, how about running your own column each week—get readers to put their problems to you and you help 'em out? You've been around a bit, Dave, and they might listen to you."

So I gave it a try. And I'll say here and now, hand on heart, that I've found it a most moving experience. For more than two years, the letters poured in. A few wanted the usual autograph or picture. But most were about very real problems. The problems of growing up, of facing up to a pretty hostile world, of everything.

And I do mean EVERYTHING! Difficulties at home with parents, loneliness, sex, capital punishment, colour prejudice, what to do if you fancy a married man, virginity, how to cope with Dirty Old Men. You name it and I've had a letter or a hundred about it.

I'll admit it started as "just another job" in what was already a very crowded week. Then the sheer responsibility of it all took over. I'd sit for hours, maybe driving to a personal appearance, wondering what to say to a girl who felt she was too ugly to face other people. How to comfort a girl who was laughed at because she was in love with a deaf boy. What on earth I could say to a girl who genuinely was threatening suicide because the world to her looked a terrible and terrifying place.

Just how DO you go about helping these people? What alarmed me most was that so many young people NEEDED someone to listen to their troubles. They couldn't, or wouldn't, go to their parents. Not even their best friends. They went on and on, worrying themselves sick, simply because they felt there was nobody to share the burden.

And an ordinary bloke like me comes along, offers a listening ear—and the mail comes in by the sack-load. All I could do was offer common-sense advice; try and put the problem in the right perspective. One week, I even addressed a column to parents—because I'm sure they have to share some of the blame for what happens to their kids.

What started out as a bit of a giggle, if you like, became something that often gave me considerable concern . . . yes, and the odd nightmare. Really I was in a position of trust, having been handed these secrets.

Of course I came in for some mickey-taking from my mates in the pop world. Some of 'em wanted to know just what gave me the right even to offer advice . .

But that wasn't the point. What mattered was that readers in trouble just wanted to SHARE their anxieties. And what pleased me was that I got letters back saying that I HAD helped . . . quite a few from mums who recognised it was THEIR daughters who had written in.

Most of all though, it made me realise that I had been really lucky, having a great family life and getting the opportunity to do just what I wanted with my own future. If you've never been lonely, then it's hard to imagine what loneliness really means.

What it adds up to is that I had a weekly platform where I could blow my top if I wanted, sympathise if I wished, provide about twelve inches of column-type shoulder to cry on.

Whatever happens, I'll never take things for granted again. I've got sack-loads of letters proving the courage, the grit, the despair, the grief, the joy of thousands of darned nice people.

The pleasure has been entirely mine. And that's a fact.

These little girls all have famous daddies (or mummies or both). Do you know who the dads are? (The answers are on page 75)

D

H

K

A

E

L

B

F

I

C

G

J

M

Whose Little Girl Are You?

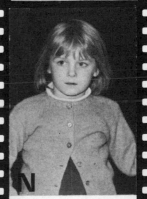

N

If you believe, like your grandad probably did, that you dream of horrible events because you ate cheese late at night, don't go on reading. If you believe, as the gipsies do, that your dream will come true, not word for word, but possibly quite reversed, read on. I may, I hope, persuade you that those fantastic stories which you experience nightly, have a different, deeper meaning.

I have collected dreams for years. I have read about them, studied them, analysed them. Our emotions, our fears and hopes, loves and hatreds shape our dreams—not that piece of cheese! Often we dream of exactly what we would like to do in real life. That's great. Often our conscience, which doesn't go completely to sleep, yells "STOP, you can't do this, not even in a dream!" Then, like writers and painters, we use symbols in order to get our story across. Whatever we dream is highly personal. It belongs to us as much as our actions in day time. These stars were nice enough to tell us what they dream and they did give away bits and pieces of their real selves, all of them.

SUSAN GEORGE

Susan George has very elaborate dreams. A recent one involved buying a pair of shoes for her sister and going downstairs to look for a friend to find he had gone to America. Then, as she walked along the road, a telephone appeared and he called to say he was at the station waiting for her.

Susan George's dream tells about her relationship with a friend. She isn't quite sure about him. Her going downstairs looks as if she has to go down to his level. She feels at times that as a person she is "high above him". So, in her dream, she sends him off to America . . . only to miss him the next morning. A telephone appears in the road and communication is swiftly re-established. Susan hears her friend is waiting at the station; a station is always a symbol for changes. Her dream ends here. Susan seems to think that whether she goes to meet him or whether he leaves without seeing her, there will be changes in this relationship.

KENNY EVERETT

Kenny Everett once dreamt that he was at a very smart garden party and he suddenly discovered how to fly. He decided to turn a somersault and then he turned another and after the third he started flying. He was zooming about above everyone's heads and they were all gazing up and looking very surprised and he was looking down on all the hats. Then he landed and he tried the three somersaults again but nothing happened.

When dreaming *Kenny* discovers suddenly that he can fly, he *wants* to get away from the smart garden party, the chit-chat, the elegant hats. He knows he belongs to a better atmosphere. So he flies away. And surprises the whole lot. But now his modesty or his conscience interfere. Looks as if Kenny is saying to himself, "Well, they aren't such a bad lot after all. And you can shock and surprise all those snobbish people once in a blue moon, but really you can't make a habit of it, can you?"

CILLA BLACK

Cilla Black says: "This is a dream I have quite a lot, and it's usually in colour. I dream that I am in a big aeroplane flying, but I don't know where to. Suddenly I get very excited because the plane is going down and down, and seems as though it's going to crash. I am not at all afraid, it's absolutely exhilarating, because just before the plane reaches the ground it starts to go upwards".

This is a beautiful dream, plucky and exciting, dreamt by a courageous and vibrant girl. Don't think that it will literally come true. It won't. If she had such a frightening trip in real life, maybe *Cilla* wouldn't be as thrilled as she is in her dream. To her, as to many others, flying stands as a symbol of loving. When Cilla loves—and I guess she is in love when this dream occurs—she does not know where she is going, where love will take her. But she is not afraid. She is loyal and when difficulties arise, when her plane is likely to crash, she becomes exhilarated. She realises that love has its crises, that they belong to it as much as high-flying moments.

These are some dreams of famous people and the possible meanings of them . . .

By DIANA HUNT

JUDITH DURHAM

Judith Durham says: "A dream I used to have quite frequently is that I am weightless—a feeling that I am on the Moon. I start to take steps, and each step I take carries me a very long way—almost as if I'm flying."

Judith's dream is typical for a public figure, an artist and a good trouper. She feels weightless, insubstantial, in a totally new world . . . on the Moon. Far away from all her friends and her family. The Moon, after all was unknown territory up to a few months ago, when those brave astronauts landed. Judith feels as if she were one of them, not quite knowing what or who will face her. She is not the only artist who finds the public unpredictable, who wonders if even fans will be kind or unkind. Her dream shows her involved relationship with her audience—she is a bit frightened, a bit in love and very defenceless and vulnerable. Well, in her dream each brave step carries her a very long way. In real life, every performance makes her more sure of herself.

STEVE ELLIS

Steve Ellis has dreamt that he walks down the road in his underwear. It is a very busy street filled with people doing their shopping, and he suddenly realises that he has an absolute minimum of clothes on. He is horrified and embarrassed and dreading the looks that people will give him when they realise, but he keeps on—as there is nowhere he can hide where there aren't just as many people—and then he realises that no one seems to be looking at him at all.

Here we have another so-called typical dream, the sensation of being half-dressed or in the nude some place where everyone else is fully dressed. *Steve Ellis'* underpants aren't meant for show and he's terribly worried parading them in a busy street. As you may be if you dream you are at a party in your nightgown. Steve, like the rest of us, cherishes his "public image", the part of his personality fit for others to see. He fears, and we all do the same that the world would be shocked or disappointed if it could see our real selves—in underwear.

ALAN WHITEHEAD

Alan Whitehead says: "Last night I dreamt that I was back during my schooldays. I had just bought a beautiful new motorbike of which I was very proud, and I took it along to school to show it off. I left it in the playground and went to find my best friend. I found him and asked him to come and see my new bike. We walked back to the playground, but when we got there the bike had changed into a car. The wheels of the car were missing, and it was all scratched and dirty. I couldn't believe it! That's all I remember."

Kids often dream of being grown up; *Alan* dreams of being a schoolboy again. He goes back to schooldays, and he wants to boast.

Looks as if Alan's conscious self tells him that he has outgrown his school friends and all childish boasting. A chapter, childhood, has come to a definite end. He has travelled very far away from it. Today he is a different and better person.

FRAZER HINES

Frazer Hines dreams that he is himself and everyone is calling him Frazer but he can see that it's not really him as he is. He starts running down a corridor that is very narrow and covered in one long mirror on either side, and it gets narrower as he runs along it. He is being chased by a man whose footsteps he can hear getting closer but when he turns round he can't see his face.

Frazer Hines' dream shows his search for his true identity. The long corridor covered with a huge mirror does not help. I think Frazer will have to do a bit of soul-searching to find his real self.

The man who chases him is a familiar figure to dreamers. It stands for a fear which exists only in our imagination but has no real substance. I don't know from whom or what Frazer is running away. I can't even guess, as I never met him. But I do know that when he faces this bogey man in daylight, Frazer will shake him off. Those faceless men of our dreams *always* vanish.

Dreams Come True

One of the great rock bands of all time . . . they just need someone to light the fuse to explode the scene all over again.

STONE AGE

Sooner or later, even the Rolling Stones will join the ranks of the unemployed, retire to their gilded halls and try to convince their kids that once they were hungry and homeless and happy playing their blues, storming the world, shaming the Establishment with their honesty.

But when? How long can their satanic majesties keep pulling the rabbit out of the hat, keeping their fans dancing when they call the tune? It would be uncharacteristic of The Stones to simply fade away; they are more likely to fragment and fall apart after a big bang. But what is there to hold them together now?

Mick (No. 1) has always held the key to The Stones' future, and as long as he wants to play with The Stones, he will shake them out of their semi-retirement for another frontal attack. But Mick may be too busy with his independent career as an actor, following his successful *Ned Kelly*, to go through all the hang-ups of going back on the road.

None of The Stones is on the breadline, although Mick Taylor isn't quite in the country estate class yet.

None of The Stones would want to be playing as the oldest rock 'n' roll band in the world. None of The Stones exist solely for the group. Bill records other groups, Charlie illustrates children's books, Keith occasionally sits in with other bands, Mick Taylor does odds and ends with other musicians, and Mick, with his complete lack of self-consciousness, cannot fail as an actor.

The two people most likely to keep the band together, are Keith and Mick Taylor. They are still learning about each other as musicians, and they are frustrated that audiences can only hear their partner-ship on records. Keith is constantly lamenting Mick's long absences filming. Okay, if that's what Mick wants, great, is Keith's attitude, but at the same time, he frets and fusses, like a hunting dog held back from its kill.

Mick Taylor has been with The Stones for more than a year now, and this could decide whether The Stones will do shows any more. For a year, an ambitious musician joining a crack band would sit tight, thank his lucky stars and just hope he fits in. Mick has been through the initiation scene, and now he can start putting in a word for himself. He wants to do all sorts of creative things out-side the group—albums with a group of his own friends will appear in time—but it will always pull hard at him that he is a member of one of the great rock bands of all time, that just needs a fuse to explode all over again.

At 21, Mick Taylor isn't ready for retirement, even though the rest of the band may feel like calling it a day. Teetotal and vegetarian, the gentle Mick Taylor, with his Rennaissance face and unassuming manner, must have seemed a strange choice to the knockers, who probably hoped for more outrages from The Stones. Because he was more like The Stones as they really are, he fitted in like the straight edge of a jigsaw. He reminds me of the intelligent students who turned out on Saturday nights to wail with The Stones in the early days, and like them, he looks to The Stones for all the answers about life that can be put into the words of a song.

It is because he knows they have the answers that he will want them to go on performing. The Stones still have something to say that deserves a bigger audience than the walls of their recording studio.

June Southworth

This is dedicated to any girl who has ever had a burning desire to be a modern dancer. To anyone who has watched the "super-group" of dance troupes, Pan's People, on Top of the Pops and said, "I could do that". Read on and see if you could.

"To be good enough for Pan's People, a dancer would need many years' training and a few years' experience. She'd need a strong but fairly slim body, and an extremely flexible frame. She'd have a fine feel for music and beat, and the ability to quickly latch on to dance routines. For most dancing work it's important to have a pretty, or at least an expressive, face."

Speaking? Flick Colby, one of the founder members of top TV modern dancing sextet, Pan's People. She's also the group's choreographer, and knows what she's talking about.

But to be like Flick Colby is not as easy as you might think. Just because you enjoy dancing at the local disco once a week, that doesn't mean you would make a successful TV dancer with no effort. You have to do ballet training!

The best age to start your training is eight, but if you're fourteen or fifteen it's not too late.

So—you're the right age, you have a natural feel for music, and you have all the ambition in the world.

Ideally, you'll go to one of the recognised stage schools where you have a normal education interspersed with frequent dancing lessons—that is, ballet lessons, to gain stamina, strong muscles, balance and control—all of which are essential.

If you can't go to a stage school you'll enrol at an ordinary dancing school (there's one in nearly every town). You'll attend at least four times a week and practise in your spare time. Training does need money, but there are few extra expenses. Anyway, you're determined, so nothing will stop you.

You've been dancing every day for at least a few years and you're around sixteen or seventeen. You feel it's time you started working. You'll go along to every audition in your area for a dancing part in panto-mime. If you're shy, you'll give up now. You'll appear in panto for three months, then before long it'll be summer season time which means another audition and another three months' work. The pay won't be marvellous, but it'll mean you'll work six months out of twelve before you've even left home. The other six months you'll spend practising every day and auditioning for any dancing part you hear of.

When you started dan-cing you may have worried because your figure wasn't too good. By now you'll have found you've developed a dancer's body—beautiful legs, a straight back, tremendous carriage, and your bust may have lost an inch or two. If you're still dedicated you won't start smoking and you'll drink alcohol rarely.

After two years you'll know whether you've made a huge mistake about being a dancer (like if you take days to learn a three-minute dance sequence) or you'll be raring to continue.

You'll pack your dancing gear and go to London, or Manchester 'cos that's where the greatest chances for dancers are. You'll find some cheap digs and set about making your mark on the dancing world of the big city.

This you'll do by getting together a composite of professional photos of you —dancing, walking, standing. That could cost you around £20. You'll compile a credit list of work you've done. You'll carry these round with you to as many auditions, agents, managers and choreographers as you possibly can, in between keeping up your daily dance practice. Choreographers and other powers-that-be prefer faces they have seen before rather than un-knowns.

You'll find all the addresses of the right people by phoning Spotlight, and you'll discover all the auditions you could wish for by reading the show-biz trade paper, The Stage, each week.

The work that will come your way at first will be cabaret, clubs, and musical stage productions if you're lucky. After one, two or more years, through sheer dedication, determination and talent you may find that you're one of those enviable dollies brightening up TV spectaculars in a famous dancing troupe.

That's what could happen. On the other hand, you could drop out and take up an office job before you've begun your career. You may never reach the top, but spend your career doing cabaret dancing. You may never earn more than £20 a week. But once you've become a dancer you'll never give up. It'll be in your blood. Dancing's like that—ask Pan's People.

THE RUNNING, JUMPING SKIPPING LIFE OF A DANCER

BY JUDITH WILLS

SO YOU WANT TO BE A DESIGNER

by MIA SCAMMELL

Move over Mary! (Quant, of course) That's the great idea of lots of people who think it's dead easy to be a fashion designer. Well, it ain't easy! The going is very tough and you've got to be determined. And so, to inspire or disillusion you completely, we've found out all you need to know! We've talked to lots of designers, and teachers at art colleges. There's only one thing to say after you've read all this — good luck!

We're starting with a realistic story, not much glamour, but it's very typical of a young designer's life.

Sue Lyon, who's 22 years old, has been designing for four years now. She left the London College of Fashion at 18 after a two year course in design. Her first job was with Frank Usher, and she gained lots of experience. Said Sue, "Through working for a top firm, like Frank Usher, who give you a basic training in mass production of dresses, anyone wishing to become a designer can fully realize every aspect of work involved in every sample designed. This experience provides a firm footing for later posts when one is the sole designer and has the responsibility of producing a range of garments."

Sue can remember the rosy pictures that were painted at college. "When the time came for us all to

find jobs, that was the big crunch. No firm—or so it seemed—wanted to take on girls without trade experience. Some of us carried on trying, others gave up and that was a big waste of talent. But you must keep

on, and try and try. Take whatever's offered, learn what you can. Then you can go on to bigger and better things. In the end it's worth it."

Sue gave a rough idea of a designer's work. "Usually one cuts the first sample pattern. The materials, trimmings, and any other work (such as pleating) must be seen to by the designer, who is also involved in the costing of a garment. That means first-hand knowledge of manufacture, and the ability to give orders to the sample machinist. Trimmings and other finishes that can make or break a design must all be taken into consideration too. It can be rather gruelling, but exciting. The work is hard and you can often feel you're getting nowhere. But suddenly, when a range of seventy to a hundred styles come to life, it's all worthwhile! You have the satisfaction of seeing what you've created."

Sue's ambition is to be really successful. At the moment she's happy, she's designing with a trendy young firm. One day, if she's rich and famous, you'll remember that you read about her first in Fabulous!

At the other end of the scale is someone who helps budding designers! **Sula Housman,** the *avante-garde* fashion merchandiser for Courtaulds, has been called the Hughie Green of fashion! She sees many hopefuls. "Such a lot come

to me with talent—but none with business sense. I've come to the conclusion, sadly, that you need to be as good at business management as you are at producing good ideas. It's so hard for freelancers, most of them end up bust because they can't cover their costs.

"You need terrific stamina, and you need backing. It's better not to start on your own but work for a firm. You have a regular wage, no headaches and financial worries."

Sula explained what she actually does: "A designer comes to me with her ideas. If I like the look of them and feel they're good, I show her the Courtaulds fabrics from which she chooses. Through me she can get fabrics from manufacturers who do not normally sell in tiny quantities. After she's produced her sample designs I get her editorial coverage and publicity (this is, of course, if her work is worth pushing) and after that the buyers come to buy the stuff.

"But I only encourage people whose designs are unusual and who really have something. I can help and bring out what they've got, but if they're only average I recommend them to get steady jobs."

Although Sula feels that "commercial firms kill ideas" she says, "You're not really free when you're working freelance. The work can be 24 hours a day, every day, and you must have a slightly commercial aspect or you go bust."

So there you have the words of wisdom from two people who know what this designing lark is all about! And here is the gen for all would be's on what you need to be a designer and how to get to college.

Before we start, let's get one thing straight. It's not just being able to draw pretty pictures! Also, before you go leaping ahead with your designs, stop and think! If you're still at school have a chat with your Careers Officer. The Youth Employment Office will also be helpful and probably give you useful leaflets too.

Right then! To be accepted on any course in fashion designing you need qualifications. Courses vary from college to college, so for a course (varying from one to three years) resulting in a college certificate you need a minimum of three G.C.E. O Levels. A three year course resulting in a Diploma in Art and Design (which is the equivalent of a degree) needs a higher standard of: five O Levels; or three O Levels and one A Level; or two O Levels and two A Levels. The more you get the better!

Honestly, there's so much competition, and it doesn't let up when you leave college either! The only way to find out exactly what your local college offers is to write to the Further Education Department of your local education office (you can easily find the address in your town hall or library).

So there you go then! If you've decided designing is for you, and you've what it takes to get on, don't forget to write off early for a prospectus and application forms or you'll miss out on being interviewed.

Finally we've been talking to some highly successful designers. Twenty-five year old **Angela Cash** (who

does Angela at London Town and the super cheap Penny Farvings range) says that it's very important to understand the business side of things. She says: "Try to be as idealistic as you like, but keep both feet firmly on the ground." An-

gela herself loves "to work in bed, at two in the morning with paper scattered around—and lots of lovely hot soup!"

Anne Green used to design Twiggy dresses with Twiggy, but now that's over she's doing the Miss "T" clobber. "If I'd left school now, I'd have never got in, let alone start to be a designer!" she said. "That's because the qualifications are getting higher. I only

had one G.C.E.! I think lots of wrong people are getting in nowadays. They're more academically minded but are not creative. Okay, so they've got G.C.E.s but they're not artistic. Of course, that's a very general statement. Some are talented."

Another young designer who's doing well is **Rodger Bass**, and he's interested in students coming out of college. "As you get older you can lose touch, but if you

get new blood which is part of the groovy scene, well, it works out better. Although I have a designer to help me, because I think two heads are better than one, I make the theme, choose the fabrics and get the line. Then we elaborate on it. This year is very soft and feminine, and I love the midi."

Well, we can't cram any more in! Do you still want to be a designer? Don't say we didn't warn you!

If you think you have fashion flair why not try designing an outfit and draw it on our model here? If you think it looks the greatest send a copy to us: Fab Annual Fashion, Fabulous 208, Fleetway House, Farringdon Street, London, E.C.4. (Enclose a s.a.e. if you want your drawing returned.)

45

DO YOU WANT TO KNOW A SECRET?

Hey, girl! Do you want to know ten secrets? Ten secrets behind the looks of ten beautiful girls from Britain, Holland, Australia and France? Then read on, 'cos we've persuaded each lovely lady to give us her personal, red-hot beauty tip. Ten secrets—just for you.

Ann Holloway (*Father, Dear Father*) 1

"Men love girls with beautiful complexions. I think if you have a fairly normal skin, the best way to ward off blemishes (and lines as you get older) is always to use soap and water to cleanse, even if you use a cream first. It's the only way *my* skin feels really clean."

Francoise Hardy 2

"One of the surest ways to attract and hold a boy is permanently to smell gorgeous. I use Vent Vert by Balmain—perfume or cologne—and in my daily bath I put Sea Water Concentrate by Revlon. It's expensive but the fragrance is worth the cost!"

Adrienne Posta 3

"If you're feeling fresh and clean you have more confidence. My favourite way to get really and truly clean (better than a normal bath) is to take a sauna bath once in a while. It makes you feel wonderful. And the best face tonic is first to steam your skin in hot water, then splash with very cold water."

Judith Durham 4

"From my experience, boys hate thick make-up. So for a smoother, more natural make-up always apply your foundation with a damp sponge. Doing it this way means your make-up won't hide your face, just enhance it. Besides, the less you use, the less the cost!"

46

Penny Spencer 5

"It's very important for a girl to have attractive, well-kept nails. I have long nails, but only because of a product I've found called *Mavala*. It's Swiss, and you can buy it for a few shillings from most chemists. You paint it on and it strengthens your nails and protects them from breaking. If a nail has already broken, use *Mavala* to hold the nail together for as long as you wish."

Sheila White 6

"This is a tip for straightening wavy hair given me by my hairdresser—especially good for longish hair. When you've washed your hair, comb it as straight as you can and pop one large roller on the crown. Taking the rest of your hair section by section, wrap it round your head very flat, using the roller as a centre, until your hair's all up like a turban. Secure with a couple of pins then tie a scarf round your head and leave until dry."

Anita Harris 7

"Beauty goes hand in hand with health, and health with sleep and relaxation. I have at least eight hours' sleep a night, plus some ten-minute feet-up periods during the day. I relax by going for a walk in the fresh air. I'm sure it's this routine that improves my hair, complexion, eyes and figure."

Mariska Veres (Shocking Blue) 8

"It's so important to take good care of your skin. It's never too early to start a thorough skin care routine. I clean my face with gentle baby soap and water every morning, then follow that with astringent and a light moisturiser. At night I nourish my skin with a cream, after making sure every trace of make-up is off."

Christine Holmes 9

"I think boys are attracted to a girl with nice eyes. To keep my eyes at their best, I eat lots of raw carrots, citrus fruits and green veg. I have plenty of sleep to ward away shadows and bags, and don't smoke or drink. I keep my eye-make-up natural, with just gloss and fluttery lashes."

Carol Dilworth 10

"A tip for blondes—wash your hair as usual then put some Borax in the rinsing water. That's an idea passed on from my mother. Doing this keeps my hair soft and shining, and I'm sure it's the reason that I'm still a natural blonde. Once when I stopped using Borax for a while my hair started to go darker."

By
Judith Wills

Cliff Richard was sitting watching *Coronation Street* a few years ago when he heard Minnie Caldwell say, "Oh I do like that chubby Cliff Richard."

It gave him a bit of a shock because he'd never thought of himself that way before but when he looked in the mirror he said to himself, "My goodness, I am chubby," and then he thought, drat, that's not the image I want to throw out.

"So I immediately cut out all bread and potatoes and lost 10 lb. in two weeks—I was 12 st. 7 lb. at the time—mind you I used to eat enormous steaks to make up for it."

Now he's down to 10 st. and intends to stay that way. But it's not easy because Cliff enjoys his food. "I love things like steamed pudding and great home-made apple crumble. I think people who tend to be fat love things like cream dougnuts.

"I'm letting you into all my trade secrets but yesterday I hadn't eaten all day and when I got home I found a Christmas pudding, cut off two slices, fried them up and ate them before going out to dinner."

While he was talking, Cliff was tucking into nothing more fattening than a bowl of leek soup. When he'd finished it, he ordered a huge lump of cheese but left most of it. He takes his slimming very seriously.

"I don't eat much during the week," he said, "but I let myself go at the weekend. Then I eat what I like. I put on three pounds last Sunday but got rid of it again by not eating on Monday. Last time I went on holiday, I put on 10 pounds."

He says he's tried all sorts of diets. "At one time I used to go around with a bag of apples and whenever I felt hungry I would eat one. I didn't eat anything else, only apples. I really used to bore people with my slimming. But I don't suppose I'd bother if I wasn't in show business."

Cliff was taking a quick break between rehearsals for his television series. He was eating at a tiny cave-like restaurant in the basement of an antique market near Baker Street.

It was one o'clock and there were plenty of people around but no one took much notice of him except a middle aged woman who wanted him to sign her leg which was in plaster after a ski-ing accident. Cliff didn't seem to mind at all.

"No, I don't mind signing autographs," he said. "I don't get tired of the fans either. It's natural to want to be liked and I enjoy it. You can't remain in show business without being an extrovert. I enjoy everything which goes with it—all the chasing around.

"My mother used to say that when you are well known, you can't go anywhere but you can, because you can afford to go to places where you're not known, like America. It's absolute rubbish to say pop stars have no privacy.

"It's a frame of mind. Of course you can do things like going into a pub. The thing to do is just to go in and have a drink. But if you walk in wearing a double breasted mink jacket obviously people treat you as something different."

Cliff is a chatty, friendly sort of person to meet, not a bit pop starish. Perhaps that's because he doesn't lead a pop star sort of life.

"I don't go to a lot of show biz parties and I really don't mix with show biz people. My closest friends are the Shadows, Una Stubbs and Norrie Paramor."

Otherwise, he says he doesn't know many other big names in pop. He hasn't seen John Lennon, for example, for about eight years. "I don't really know him. I wouldn't like to make any decision about him. I only know what I read about him and you can't always tell from that.

"But the days are certainly gone when the Beatles used to go into the kitchen at parties strumming their guitars and saying, 'This is going to be our next record'.

"Of course I could lead a totally show biz life if I wanted to but I like to get out and meet people who have nothing to do with show business. I find there's a lot of reality outside.

"When I'm at home, I visit my neighbours' houses. Of course it takes time before they treat me as an ordinary person but you can't expect to be treated normally straight away."

Cliff, who was 30 in October, lives in a quiet, almost countryfied part of North London. He shares his house with a friend and the friend's mother. It's a fairly large, detached house with a lawn in front and a small drive but by pop standards it's pretty modest.

Occasionally the odd fan manages to track him down, but Cliff is rather proud of the fact that he made his latest move without any publicity at all.

"Most people don't know where I live and some fans go to my old house, thinking I still live there."

Most of his neighbours are middle-aged with grown up children but it's the sort of atmosphere which suits him. He goes to their parties and they visit him and it's a good change from the sort of life he normally leads.

When he's at home in the evenings, he says he likes to potter around or watch television—his favourite programmes being *I Spy, Bugs Bunny* and the *David Frost* interviews. He also writes songs.

"But no one will ever hear them, they're not good enough," he said. He belongs to a local badminton club and plays there when he gets time.

"If I'm not working on Saturday mornings, I run a football club at the local Crusaders, I've been doing that for four years now. I get some of my rudest criticism from the kids but it's good to feel they can be honest with me."

After his television series finished Cliff played in *Five Finger Exercise*. It's a straight, serious play and Cliff's part was difficult.

"I want to act very much and we let this fact be known. When I was offered the part I thought, well, I may as well jump in the deep end.

"But I'll never give up pop. I love it. Singing is the easiest thing for me next to getting out of bed. But I find acting very fulfilling. No singer has managed to bridge the gap between pop and the theatre and I want to be the first to do so."

Once he was 12 stone 7 lbs and hated the "chubby Cliff" image so he systematically lost two and half stones . . . but he still longs for cream doughnuts and home-made apple crumble!

A Little Less of Cliff!

TONY BURROWS by Steve Campbell

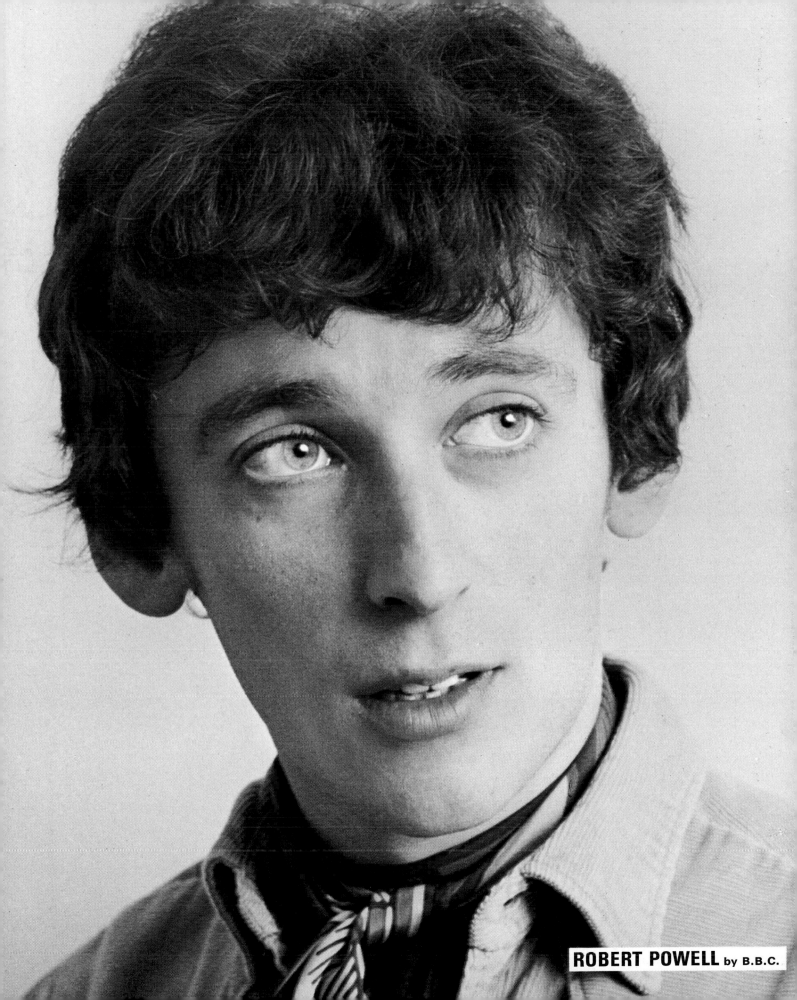

ROBERT POWELL by B.B.C.

YOUR TOP TWO TV SERIES

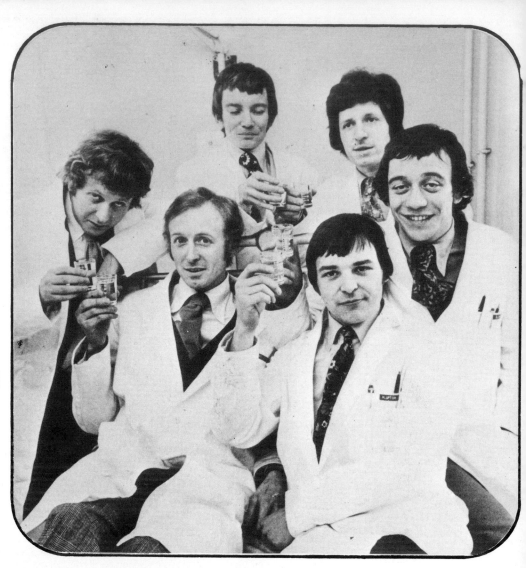

What assets does a TV series need to win your vote as favourite series of 1969/1970? That is the question. We've put on our thinking caps (hand-knitted, of course) and arrived at this formula:
Top TV series=

Lots of dishy young men plus a dolly girl or two plus comedy plus pace plus originality plus entertaining story-line.

That's a good deal to ask of a TV show, but two series, both on TV regularly during the past year, have all these qualities plus more. No wonder everyone from six to sixty loved them! The names of these shows — *Doctor in the House* and *Please Sir!* of course.

Doctor in the House was first screened one Saturday night in late 1969 — and two weeks after it's initial appearance the postman at London Weekend Television threatened to strike 'cos he could hardly lift the bulging, heavy sacks of mail all addressed to the series! Here are the ingredients that go towards making *Doctor in the House* your top TV series number one.

Plenty of super men in the shape of Duncan Waring (Robin Nedwell); cheeky Northerner Paul Collier (George Layton); Dave Briddock (blond Simon Cuff); the cool Dick Stuart-Clark (Geoffrey Davies); Welshman Huw Evans (Martin Shaw); Danny Hooley (Jonothan Lynn) and your favourite actor of the year, handsome Barry Evans as Michael Upton.

Comedy packaged in the form of Upton and Waring with Layton always around to help. Pace — you could almost miss every other witticism or mad caper if you laughed too long at the first. And there was always at least one dishy girl around for the fellas. Which all most definitely adds up to an original, entertaining show. Three cheers for scriptwriters Graham Chapman and Barry Cryer.

Please, Sir!

Question — during the last twelve months, what TV series was it that made telly-viewers forget about helping to wash the car or do the gardening each Sunday afternoon? And what show was guaranteed to keep people glued to the TV every Saturday night it was on? Answer — *Please, Sir!* Let's see just what it was that made *Please, Sir!* your Top TV series number two.

Take an ordinary classroom in a typical secondary modern school, called Fenn Street, and a class full of fifth-year pupils, and you have a situation anyone who has ever been to school can identify with. But watch *Please, Sir!* for a while and you realise that the pupils do and say all the things you would love to do at school, but never dared. That's part of its popularity.

The rest is — Abbott, the sheep in wolves' clothing (David Barry); rough, tough Duffy (Peter Cleall); endearing Dunstable (Peter Denyer); smooth guy Craven (Malcolm McFee); and "Sir" himself — long-suffering Bernard Hedges played by amiable John Alderton. For the male viewers there was sexy Sharon (Penny Spencer) and maternal Maureen

(Liz Gebhardt.) Put all those in one classroom and you are bound to have comedy and pace. Add Potter the caretaker bantering with Hedges, Hedges bantering with the other teachers and what do you have but top TV show number two. And congrats to London Weekend Television for screening both *Doctor in the House* and *Please, Sir!*

Judith Wills.

53

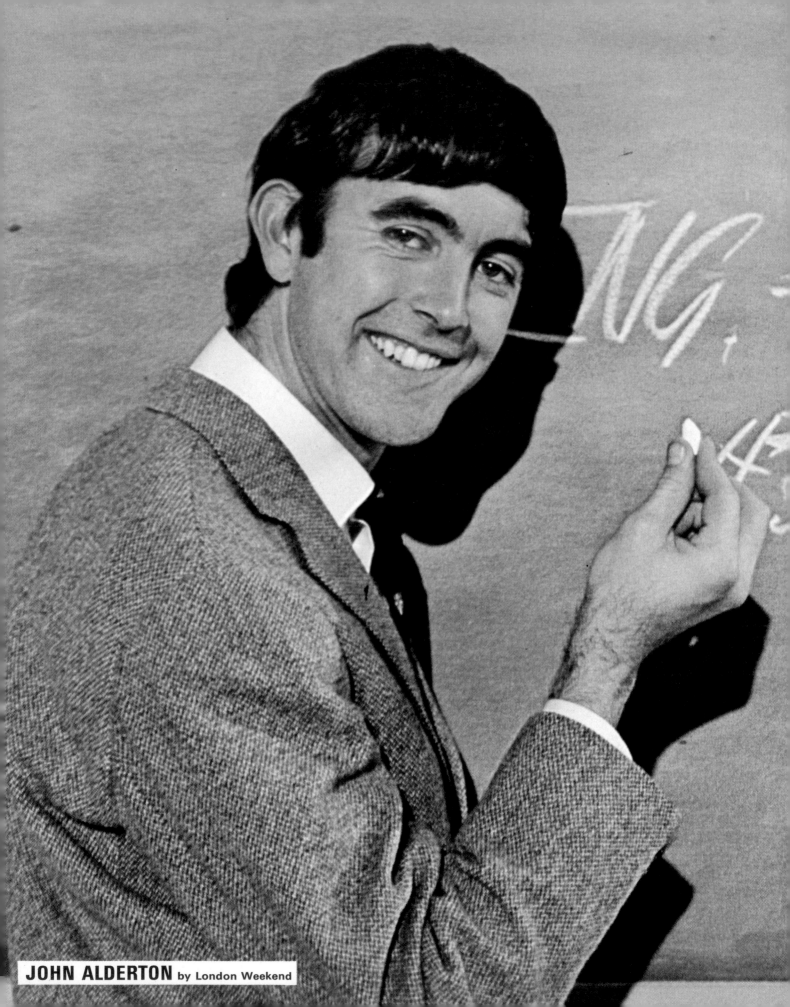

JOHN ALDERTON by London Weekend

BARRY EVANS by Peter Pugh-Cook

He has come a long way from the days when he answered to the number 3188 in a Californian reform school.

"What I've got is mine," say Steve McQueen with th defiance of a self-made ma of property. "I made it."

Proud words those from proud man. A man who ha got what he wants and doesn intend to part with it.

For such is Steve McQueer

He has come a long wa from the days when he an swered to the number 318 in a Californian reform schoo Most of his fans, who pape their walls with photograph of his ruggedly handsome face would disregard as irrelevar those two years when th young McQueen was deeme "incorrigible".

But he has not forgotten.

Often in interviews he re minds people of his past. H drags up his record and run through an outline of his varie career, his wild days as lumberjack, a seaman, a fair ground barker, even as a run ner for a brothel.

It is a dramatic story, it bear telling, and it gives more tha a hint of what has made hir the sort of man he is.

For though he has bee adopted by Hollywood, ac cepted for his ability as a actor, and become famed as a international idol, Steve Mc Queen has never been tamec

Try as they might no one wi ever cast the shroud of respec

STEVE MCQUEEN
BRAVE, BOLD, DEFIANT

ability around his powerful frame. He was born a tough guy. Nothing will change that.

He himself has fought and will continue to fight to ensure that he is not ensnared and softened by the easy life.

"This is a tough business," he says. "You take a man off the streets and make him famous and he loses all sense of values."

That is why no one does the stunts for this actor. If there is a particularly hairy scene to be filmed—and there are lots—it is McQueen himself who goes before the cameras.

Perhaps it is his daring and his personal courage which endear him to many people. Today's film fans don't want a plastic hero, a "Celluloid" star, the sort of actor of whom it is whispered that off-screen he actually can't bear the sound of gun fire.

And when the particular hero is McQueen, they know he is not just a pretty face with curly blond hair, blue eyes and a passable talent for acting. He has proved himself to be a Real Man.

On his part it is in fact quite a considerable achievement to have shone through the sycophantic burblings of the publicity which has naturally adhered to his antics.

For his character has emerged not only as a toughie, but as someone of honesty and integrity who really does care about life outside his immediate environment.

He has shown that he still has time for others, and he has managed to gain for himself the reputation of being one of the nicest guys you could hope to meet.

Steve McQueen is nearly 40. He is closer in age to the parents of his fans than he is to the kids themselves. Yet he has always been able to iden-

tify with the young.

It is not something that he has done merely by driving fast cars and risking his life. It is not even that he has been caught up in a business which too often capitalizes on youth. It is not an image that has been built for him.

Trying to explain it himself recently he said he thought it was perhaps because he has been fighting the establishment all his life. On another occasion he has attributed it to his interpretation of the characters he has played on screen.

But I think the point is that he stands—as a man, not as an actor—for so much that the young themselves stand for today. He has lived his life the way he has wanted to with no reference to protocol. He has been successful but has never allowed it to blur his vision of his ideals.

He has kicked at conventions, cocked a snook at the pretensions of the establishment, and he has got away with it.

He has been honest, too, about his need for something extra to give him the thrill of excitement that success as an actor has taken away. Now that he has enough money never to need again, never to have to fight for material things, there is something missing. He still wants danger.

"The way I see it," he says, time and again, "a guy needs obstacles to keep him going."

So he creates his own obstacles by indulging a desire for speed, and racing in cars and on motor bikes.

"Acting," he explains philosophically, "is something you do with other people. Motor racing is something you do alone."

Studio chiefs, it is rumoured,

have nearly suffered heart attacks at the prospect of losing one of the film world's hottest properties as a result of McQueen's casual indifference to his own safety.

But no one except his wife, Neile Adams, has ever had any success in trying to reason with him on the subject of speed.

"My wife doesn't like it," he says, "but she puts up with it.

"Just the same a couple of years ago she took me on one side and swore at me and said for me to cut down. So I have."

He has been happily married now for over 13 years. His wife walked into a restaurant one day, he followed her out, and with delightful impulsiveness they just went and got married.

She deserves decorating, he says, for staying with him and tolerating his career and his hobby without jealousy.

"I have been let down too much and let down too often to trust people much. But the lady I married has helped quite a bit."

He always refers to her as "the old lady". She doesn't seem to mind.

"Steve's way of life is something that you just have to get used to," she says with cheerful resignation.

She is repaid for her tolerance, though, by her husband's obvious devotion and loyalty. Once asked what the best present was that he had ever received, he replied: "A little loving from the old lady."

That is not a very tough answer. But Steve McQueen is human, too.

Jane Crombie

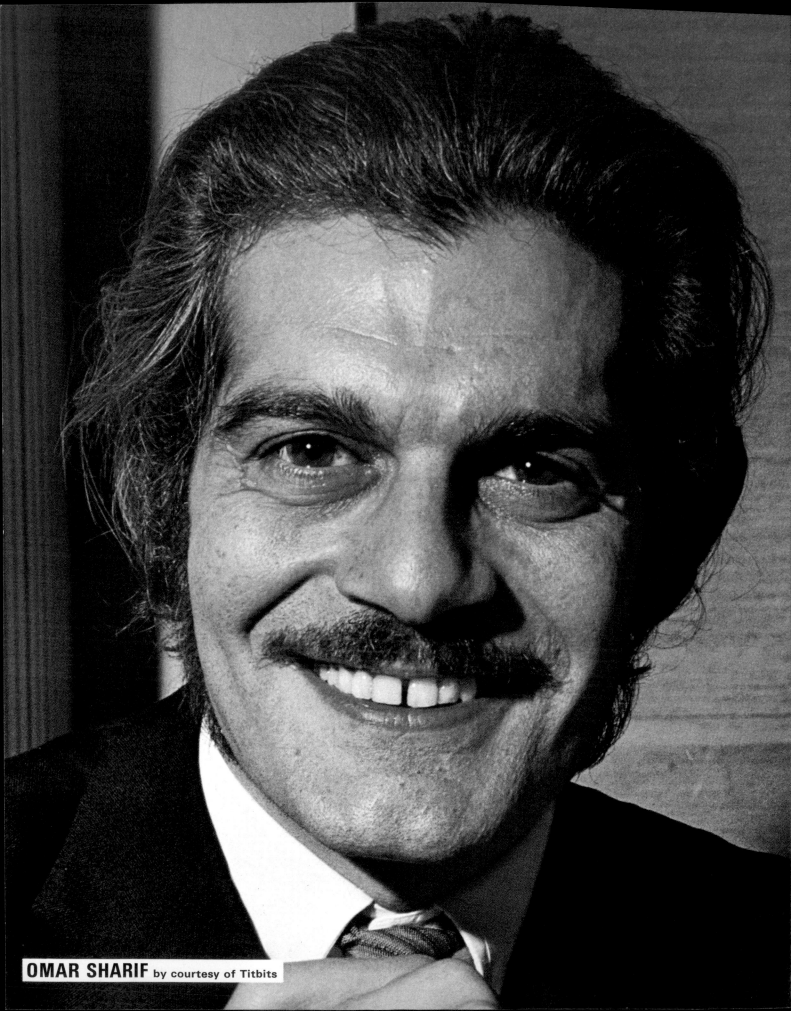

OMAR SHARIF by courtesy of Titbits

STEVE McQUEEN by L.P.A. International

PETER TORK

DOUG McCLURE

LEN NIMOY

MARK SLADE

HENRY DARROW

Hollywood is sunshine most of the time with palm trees and stars' names on the sidewalks. This is where you are likely to see Jim Stacy, Wayne Maunder, Henry Darrow or Mark Slade driving down your street or eating at the restaurant on your corner. This is the home of FAB's American Correspondent . . .

IN THE immortal words of John Lennon, we all shine on. And somehow, I can't think of a better way to describe what it's like to live in Hollywood.

Hollywood is sunshine most of the year with sometimes a little and sometimes too much rain in the winter. And it's palm trees and nearby stretches of long, sandy beach. It's stars' names on the sidewalks and stars' footprints at Grauman's Chinese theatre.

It's an "industry" town where so many of the people you meet work in entertainment as everything from prop men to vice-presidents.

It's staying up late and getting up late when you aren't working, and going to bed early and getting up earlier when you are.

It's all night coffee shops and rock-and-roll groups practising in the house next door, if not your own house.

But most of all, it's karma. Everything that has ever happened to and in this town (and a town it is because the big-city atmosphere just

doesn't exist) has remained a part of it.

Today, living in Hollywood and loving it is joining the thousands of others who are inside its aura. And it has an aura like no other place in the world.

It has within its karma, still shining on, the greatest talents in history. The stars of the silents, then the talkies, then the motion picture spectacular. It has **Clark Gable** and **Theda Bara** and **Rudolph Valentino** and **W. C. Fields** and a legion more.

Hollywood is all-night television (one channel stays on and shows some great and some ghastly oldies), and never having to get dressed up to go anywhere, even church.

Hollywood is running into your favourite star at the market, in his cut-offs and sandals, buying a dozen eggs and a jar of pickles.

Hollywood is running into your favourite star in your favourite shop where they sell wonderful things like candles and incense and kites and long silky scarves.

Hollywood is **John Barrymore**, and the blazing nightclubs on the Sunset Strip during the thirties and forties, and **Errol Flynn**, and symphonies or **Beatles** under the stars in Hollywood Bowl.

Hollywood is the weather never getting cold, the smell of jasmine trees, the sprawling movie studios with their own water tanks pointing at the sky.

Hollywood is also everything and everyone that is happening now. The names have changed, but the karma remains the same—strong, exciting and with the best of all possible vibrations.

Today it is a new crop of young people, actors and actresses doing their own thing. The liquor consumption is down incredibly and wine sells better now where gin used to flow from bathtubs (and sometimes fountains in the stars' homes). The nightclubs are all but extinct, with only a few remaining and those are private clubs like the Daisy, the Factory. Not many of the younger stars frequent these places. **Doug McClure** is a

CLARK GABLE

ERROL FLYNN

BRENDAN BOONE　　　　**DAVY JONES**

WAYNE MAUNDER

MICKY DOLENZ

clubgoer, so are several others, but the general form of entertainment is parties at home, friends in for dinner, decorating your house, sewing or designing clothes, good conversation, and going to the Troubador to hear good, good music.

With most of the film studios outside the town, like Universal in Universal City (also in the San Fernando valley where so many of todays' stars make their homes) and M-G-M in Culver City, the only two super favourites in England that are filmed right in Hollywood are "Lancer" and "High Chaparral."

This is why you are likely to see **Jim Stacy** or **Wayne Maunder** or **Henry Darrow** or **Mark Slade** driving down your street or eating at the restaurant on your corner. Out in the just-mentioned Valley it's the same thing—you can easily run into **Jim Drury. Doug McClure, Steve McQueen** (Hollywood is meeting him at a motorcycle store and talking shop for hours).

Or take a trip along Laurel Canyon which begins at the Strip and winds and twists its way through the hills to the Valley. There you'll find log cabins and beautiful houses and **Monkees** and other beautiful people.

Toward the beach, past Beverly Hills, which is not the Mecca for young stars of today, you'll find more **Monkees, Elvis Presley, Len Nimoy, Brendan Boone**.

Hollywood today is not being phoney and not wearing diamonds and furs and driving a Volkswagen or a Dune Buggy. Hollywood is living here or visiting and adding new people, new ideas, new ways to its karma, and knowing that it will still be even stronger and more exciting when you have finished your thing and gone to that Big Casting Office in the sky.

That's the Hollywood I'm happy I live in.

Janey Milstead

SUNSHINE CITY

JAMES STACY　　　　**RUDOLPH VALENTINO**

Mark Slade
Robert Wagner

James Stacy
Chris Carey

Cesare Danova
Brendon Boone

Henry Darrow

Leonard Nimoy

Andy Williams

Wayne Maunder

James MacArthur

Rudy Solari

Nearly ten years ago, Cliff sang that we should live and love while we can because we may not be The Young Ones very long. This year, Cliff is 30, and he and the ones who were loved alongside him move out of the age of the very young. But not out of their hearts. For a man who is lovable at 20 is even more lovable at 30 . . . and 40 . . . and 50. A man of beauty is a joy forever!

A BEATLE at 30 is hard to believe. A milestone for us all. Proof that time does not stop still, even for the young; proof that there is no generation gap carrying those we love into the realms of "them" as soon as the clock strikes 30; proof that 30 can be a beginning rather than an end.

Before the first year of the Seventies shuffles off into the archives, **Ringo** and **John**, according to their official biographies, will be 30, elderly as idols go. But were they more attractive at 20? I hardly think so. Ringo was The Nose, who sat at the back, and felt such an underdog that he bit the hand that fed him, blunt to the point of rudeness to fans who tried to be his friend. At 30, Ringo enjoys solo success as an actor, is a responsible family man, and is ten times more fanciable. John at 20 was violent, cynical and rootless. Now

Yoko has given him roots, peace has replaced war, and ego has given way to idealism. John has grown up.

When **Elvis** reached his thirtieth birthday there was much wailing and gnashing of teeth, as though old age would carry him off before he could give another twitch of the pelvis. Now, at 35, he's sexier than ever. The smoky eyes still burn, the sensuous lips still curl away from the white even teeth, and if you don't mind walking one pace behind his buddies—the Memphis Mafia, as they are unkindly called!—you can still get into The King's court if you are young and beautiful.

Walking one pace behind is the sort of sacrifice you must make if you fall for one of the mature toughie types who swagger into punch-ups as casually as they cut into the king-sized steaks that presumably give them the energy

in the first place. **Steve McQueen**, at 40, has the nervous energy of a caged tiger which has walked on the wild side. Screaming around Le Mans in a Porsche with Jackie Stewart, he is a hero of the Seventies, ruthlessly efficient and coolly confident. Speed is his god. His wife, actress Neile Adams, his two children, and his car are its disciples. One car accident has left him deaf in one ear, and another broke his nose, but he races on. **Dennis Hopper**, 36, another one from the cool school, races a motor bike as if it's a Porsche.

Charlie Bronson, the-man-you-love-to-hate type of screen toughie, looks, with his forever open-necked shirts, straggly moustache, narrowed eyes and widened grin, like a deserter from Pancho Villa's mob. Married to actress Jill Ireland, ex-wife of another wantable over-30, **David McCallum**, Charlie is the sort of bandit girls would want to be ambushed by on a dark night. **Lee Marvin**, downright 'ornery in films, and a singer cruelly known as "the frog with the man in his throat", is the rough protector who would probably amble to the rescue and break up the whole scene with one chorus of *Wand'rin' Star*!

Smoother by far in the strong man league is **Paul Newman**. His wife Joanne Woodward laughingly protests that he's an old married man who snores, but that

won't keep the she-wolves away from the door. We know when we're on to a good thing! I once won 10s 6d from a film magazine when they printed a letter in which I claimed Paul Newman had the most exciting eyes that ever lit up the silver screen. I don't think I was overpaid. The British equivalent to Paul Newman could be **Patrick McGoohan**, but *he* would get my vote for the most exciting voice. That crisp, clipped accent from nowhere-in-particular (actually, it's from Sheffield, via Ireland, via America) gives him a man-of-the-world mystique that always leaves a question mark trailing in his wake.

Other danger men of note—the danger being that we lose our hearts to them—also came via Ireland. Ever since **Peter O'Toole** arrived on the horizon of Arabia as Lawrence I have been unable to look at a camel without seeing a vision of O'Toole atop. I look at any passing camel trains whenever I can. **Richard Harris** supplies the blarney on TV talk shows at the drop of the hard stuff, but he is much, much more than an Irishman with the gift of the gab. Go to see *Camelot* for **David Hemmings**, if you must, but if you have any soul at all, it is Richard's Arthur which will stay with you . . . sexy, yes, but so sensitive.

ROGER MOORE

CLIFF

DUSTIN HOFFMAN

SACHA DISTEL

DAVID HEMMINGS

PETER O'TOOLE

OMAR SHARIF

PAUL NEWMAN

RICHARD HARRIS

So Old- & So Fanciable

Traditional Great Lovers never emerge before thirty. Their whole appeal is based on their experience with women. They know how to make a girl feel cherished. **Omar Sharif**, for instance, wouldn't tell you he couldn't keep a date because he was off to the pub with the lads. In *Funny Girl*, he *was* Nick Arnstein, a man you would follow halfway across the world to be with. His charm is a sort of joke between himself and the girl who falls for it, as if he acts out the girl's dream of The Great Lover. Not as a star to the starstruck, but as one human being to another. As if his place in life is to reassure us all that knights on white chargers still exist.

Sacha Distel is doing much the same thing with a French accent. I have a Sacha Distel record which is all about a Miss Someone who makes him feel so *S-E-X-Y*, with more sighs and pauses to the rpm than all of the Jane Birkin–Serge Gainsbourg records put together. Listen to *that* then try to believe him when he says he is just a family man and can't understand what women see in him.

British Great Lovers are hidden under several layers of cool, but one slow-burner who melts on contact is **Peter Wyngarde**, the King of *Department S*. Apart from the Fu Manchu moustache, he is so terribly English, with that rich mahogany voice and curling sideburns, that he should be held up to the world as an example of the sophisticated English romantic. And if that doesn't convince people that the Englishman is as sexy as any other, we could always back up our offer with **Roger Moore** and **Alan Bates**. Over 30? Yes. Past their best? No, no, no.

America would be able to produce **Richard Chamberlain** as evidence of the American romantic, but having monopolised him for the last two years, I think we should be able to claim him as our own. *Portrait of a Lady* proved to be a portrait of a gentleman called Richard Chamberlain who had improved beyond belief on his *Dr. Kildare* image, which was too clinical by half. The new, warmer Dick, complete with updated hairdo, is much more promising.

There are few men of 30 who haven't improved with age. Experience writes its lines on their faces, giving them a character they never possessed in their untouched youth. Men who are beautiful on the inside are always beautiful on the out. **Andy Williams** is 40 this year, and his fans are any age. Once, at the Royal Albert Hall, I expected to see a middle-aged audience at an Andy Williams concert, and arrived to find the place packed with fainting females. Everyone sang along with him on *In The Summertime* until tears were rolling down our faces, and our hands were falling apart from the clapping. It was fun, it was warm, it was real. After the show, I'm sure everyone in the audience wanted to send him a note to say thank you.

And then there is Cliff, thirty this year, and looking seventeen. No sighing and sobbing, please. Like all the other grown-up choirboy types (**Gene Pitney, Dustin Hoffman** and **Tommy Steele**, for instance) he is innately good and incorruptible, and the clean living has paid dividends in his face, which looks as innocent as it did when he set out on the pop path. He has reached 30 so gracefully it must give new heart to all those people clinging desperately to the twenties.

Boys are fun to be with, but they tend to relegate girls to second place behind football, cars and beer. Can you blame us for looking towards the older man who understands that a girl needs to be swept off her feet?

June Southworth

RICHARD CHAMBERLAIN

ELVIS

ALAN BATES

ANDY WILLIAMS

CHARLIE BRONSON

LEE MARVIN

RINGO

DENNIS HOPPER

PATRICK McGOOHAN

STEVE McQUEEN

Jumping Judas Food

Judas Jump have all the ingredients for a super group. But making good sounds and playing good gigs takes lots of energy and sometimes leaves very little time for meals. So we asked each of the group for their favourite quick, nourishing recipe.

Charlie Harrison (bass) has simple tastes. He loves fried steak which his mum cooks for him when he goes home 'cos she thinks he looks under-nourished! He prefers it medium rare, cooked on both sides for about 30 seconds in a really hot pan to seal the flavour and then 3–4 minutes each side on a low heat, served with chips and tomatoes.

Adrian (harmonica) is a pancake addict, and especially likes them with cream and maple syrup.

½ lb. plain flour
¼ teaspoon salt
1 level teaspoon bicarbonate of soda
1 level teaspoon cream of tartar
1 dessertspoonful of golden syrup
½ pint of milk with a teaspoon of vinegar
1 egg beaten well.

Mix the syrup and the egg together, gradually add sifted flour, bicarb., cream of tartar, salt, alternately with the milk. Beat well. Cook in very hot, greased pan. (Serves four)

Alan Jones (tenor/baritone/flute) can never eat enough corn-on-the-cob. These are very easy as you just boil them in salted water for about ten minutes and serve with lots of butter, either alone or as a vegetable with meat.

(Alan and Trevor share a flat and when they have time on Sundays they cook a big beef joint, and Trevor eats it hot with cabbage, roast potatoes and batter pudding, while Alan waits till it's cold and makes a huge salad to go with it.)

Andy Bown (guitar/organ) is vegetarian so he gets a lot of his favourite food from Cranks. He loves Pizza.

DOUGH Make bread dough to standard recipe with 8 oz. plain flour and 2 teaspoons dried yeast.

TOPPING
12 oz. tomatoes
1 large onion
1 clove garlic
1 tablespoon oil
½ teaspoon dried mixed herbs
1 teaspoon sugar
salt and pepper
2 oz. tin of anchovies
2–3 oz. black olives
2 oz. grated Parmesan cheese.

Topping: Put the tomatoes into a bowl, cover with boiling water and leave for a couple of minutes. Drain, peel and chop the tomatoes. Peel and chop the onion, peel and finely chop the garlic. Heat the oil in a pan and fry the onion and garlic till golden. Add the tomatoes, herbs, sugar, salt and pepper. Bring to the boil and simmer for 15 minutes. Turn the mixture on to the bread dough. Arrange the anchovies on top to form a lattice pattern and dot the olives between. Sprinkle with Parmesan cheese. Bake in a hot oven for 25–30 minutes.

Trevor Williams (guitar) often goes to the Swiss Centre and has developed a taste for Cheese Fondue. This is an English version which is super for a snack when you have friends in or are giving a party.

1 clove of garlic
2 oz. butter
3 level tablespoons plain flour
¾ pint of white wine
1 lb. Cheddar cheese
¼ lb. Gruyère cheese
½ teaspoon grated nutmeg
salt and pepper.

Use a heatproof earthenware dish or a saucepan. Peel and halve the garlic, rub round the inside of the dish. Melt butter in the pan and take off the heat and stir in flour. Add the wine and stir on a gentle heat till it comes to the boil. Simmer for a few minutes and remove from heat. Grate the cheese or cut it into strips and stir it slowly in while the pan is over gentle heat. Stir all the time and don't allow to boil. Season and sprinkle with nutmeg. Chop up small pieces of French bread and dip in on forks.
(Serves about six)

Predictably, drummer **Henry Spinetti's** favourite dish is Spaghetti Bolognaise.

8 oz. spaghetti
1 oz. butter
3 pints salted water.

SAUCE
2 oz. streaky bacon
2 medium sized onions
2 tablespoons oil
1 lb. lean minced beef
2 sticks celery
1 clove garlic
large pinch dried mixed herbs
2 teaspoons salt
½ teaspoon sugar
pinch black pepper
1 can tomato puree
½ pint water
Parmesan cheese.

Remove rind and cut bacon into pieces. Peel and chop onions. Heat oil in a pan and slowly fry bacon, onions, and beef until brown, stirring frequently. Chop the celery and peel and finely chop garlic. Add to the meat and onion with the remaining ingredients (except Parmesan cheese). Cover and simmer for 40 minutes.

Boil spaghetti rapidly for about 12 minutes. Drain and toss in the butter. Serve with sauce and Parmesan.

TASTY

He is an actor's actor, but first and foremost he's a top box office draw.

The reason could be that he relies on sheer, concentrated talent to hold your attention right through a film. It could be that although *you* know he's brilliant, *he* doesn't seem to realise. He's not conceited about his success but humble. He's quietly confident, not forever shouting to the world to look how great he is.

The reason could be that he's a master of contrasts. That's apparent from the three leading screen roles which rocketed him from Broadway to a "superstar" tag from the movie world. He won an Academy Award nomination for his role as the fumbling, embarrassed all-American boy, Ben, in *The Graduate*. He portrayed Ben so brilliantly that we couldn't visualise the man in any other role. Until we saw *Midnight Cowboy*. The contrast was amazing. He was suddenly an ugly, filthy, friendless con-man from his hunch-back right down to his scruffy boots. We were all busy despising the guy when *John and Mary* arrived. And he'd changed again—to a clean, confident bachelor with a well-paid job and a lovely girlfriend—Mia Farrow. Wonder what he'll turn up as next?

Almost forgot to tell you his name. Dustin Hoffman—as if you didn't know.

as Ben in The Graduate, at his post-college party . . .

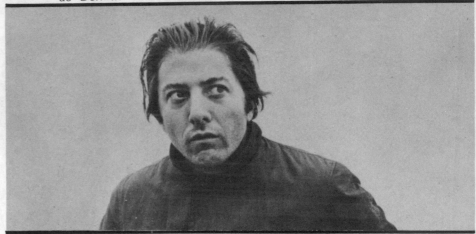

the scruffy, lonely con-man in Midnight Cowboy . . .

he's the self-sufficient, friendly bachelor in John and Mary.

TWO

as the determined ski champion in Downhill Racer . . .

the persevering Cooper in Tell Them Willie Boy is Here . . .

with Paul Newman as Butch Cassidy, here's Robert as The Sundance Kid.

I saw *Butch Cassidy and the Sundance Kid* four times. The reason was a superb, six-foot, blond, blue-eyed male—Robert Redford. The brand of handsome that makes you want to jump right into that cinema screen and be with the man. Those smouldering blue eyes that glint and invite, and suddenly you wish you'd been an actress. The kind of face you've been dreaming of ever since you fancied the boy next door when you were eight.

And now he's here. First in 1969 as a ski champion in Paramount's *Downhill Racer*—*almost* wholesome, devastatingly athletic, every inch the strong sportsman. *Tell Them Willie Boy is Here* came along in early 1970, from Universal. Mr. Redford gaining fans by the gross as Under-Sheriff of Banning, Christopher Cooper. This guy is at home on a horse and wielding a gun, too.

Then, as if our hearts weren't beating too fast already, 20th Century Fox gave us *Butch Cassidy and the Sundance Kid*. The coup. The final blow to those who had resisted Robert till then. As the Sundance Kid he was more handsome, wittier, more cool, quicker with a gun, more dashing than he'd ever been before. What chance does a mere girl have? Those eyes, that hair, that voice. . . . Say no more.

Judith Wills **69**

To Badfinger from Helena of Czechoslovakia.

I would like to be a fan of the badfinger but sorry. We are the socialist country how do you know and we can't have any English money money. This is very bad, very much and I haven't any English shilings.

To Jack Wild from Allison of Puerto Rico.

Dear Jack,

I saw you in your role The Artful Dodger andlike E/ everyone of my friends I think you are a DOLL. However, you do not look like you are 15 so we said oh, he is much to young for us. (We are 13½) I will tell you about myself - I am 4 ft. 11in. I have blonde hair (short), big green eyes, and an olive complexion. I am 32½,21,30. I like stamp collecti ng, swimm ag, tennis, and my favorite sport is horseback riding. I have 3 horses- Yankee, Gumdrop, and Pinto. I also play the piano. Iam a good student. My average is 98½ %

To Dave Clark from Mary of New York.

Luv is the scarf nice and warm that I made you. I've knitted all my love into it. I was very proud of it. Some thing I had made for you.

To Jack Wild from Asada of Japan.

Dear Mr Jack Wild,

I'm 15, Japanese girl and your fan. Since I saw "Oliver" I have been quite fascinated by you. I said to my father "Hey. Father. By all means I will find and win a boy friend like Jack Wild and marry him".

To Judas Jump from Dani of E.?.

MY WILL
IN THE EVENT OF DEATH, PLEASE PASS ALL MY WEALTH TO
JUDAS JUMP

To the Equals from Russ and Mall of Dewsbury.

Thank John for throwing his shirt into our hands from the stage, its a perfect fit and priceless. next time we're hoping Ou will throw his black polo neck jumper

To Peter Wyngarde from Helen of Horley.

I rang up the Telephone Exchange but they could not help me because you are X- Directory. I do advise you to put your name in the 'phone book I saves such a lot of trouble. You must now think me a very rude girl, but I don't mean to be. I'm a great fan of yours, so is my mum, and my grandmother!

To Kenneth Cope from Sara of N.W.9.

I missed you on T.V. last week cos just as you were starting my feller decided to dash of to the 59 and he draged me off with him. Was I mad by but you know how it is, after all he is my boy friend and your not are you

LETTER TO A STAR

To George of Edison Lighthouse from Angie of Grimsby.

...wherever your
in Grimsby come and see me and I'll
show you all the pictures I have of
you and what I've done with them

To Peter Wyngarde from Ann of Rushdean.

He's just a
regular in perfect humor with a difference.
Please will you send me some photo's and
details about him and I will be a fan forever.
I love his sideboards and moustache. I'll send some
real killer for Christmas

To the Casuals from Jeffrey in Scotland.

I AM EIGHT
YEARS OLD. PLEASE
CAN I BE THE
DRUMMER WHEN I
GET DRUMS FOR MY
CHRISTMAS. AND PLAY
THE DRUMS WHEN HE
IS ON HOLIDAYS IN
YOUR GROUP PLEASE
LOVE.
JEFFREY

To Peter Wyngarde from A. Fanatic and Heather of Preston.

I'm 5 ft tall weigh 6 stone & will do any
thing (within reason) for /to/ with you.
(cross out the ones that do not apply)
Could you send me a lock of hair,
leftovers from dinner, nail clippings, dentures,
old toothbrushes, hairy boiled sweets —
anything of yours.

I often go to the local dance
hall and my dream would
come true if I could see
you and talk about our
future. **To Stuart of Edison Lighthouse from Jane in Clapton.**

To Ray of Edison Lighthouse from Khristina of Sweden.

I am Swedish and
very lonely in England
I think he might be
very much fun together
and play games
of different kinds
because I love you.

To Peter Wyngarde from Janet of Birkenhead.

(I wish he was a
lot younger) like myself. I'm 13.

**Have you ever written to a famous personality telling
him how great you think he is? He'd love to hear from
you, you know. Fan letters are life blood to stars. The
letters here are some of the favourites lent to us by the
stars.**

Mariska Veres of Shocking Blue likes tall men, at least 5 ft. 11 in. She prefers them to be intellectual but energetic, sporting types as well if she can find a combination of the two. They must be witty, and sophisticated both in manner and appearance. She loves horror films and did say Boris Karloff looked like one of her ideal men, but settled for dishy *Christopher Lee!*

Adrienne Posta goes for men with brown hair and green eyes, and doesn't like them to be too tall as she is only 4 ft. 11 in. Her man must have a very strong personality otherwise she tends to dominate him, and she likes to know who's boss sometimes. He should laugh at the same things, have a mad sort of humour. Clothes are very important, she says, plain dark shirts and trousers with a well-cut jacket; bright T-shirts and big belts really turn her off. Ade has always liked the look of *Dustin Hoffman.*

Anita Harris says good looks aren't absolutely necessary but they certainly help! Her man should be very sensitive to others' feelings, tall and nearly always dark-haired. She likes generosity—for example when tipping—but not flashiness with money. Her ideal could well be *Sacha Distel.*

MAD ABOUT MEN!

If you think about all the boys you go out with you'll probably find that certain characteristics attract you. We asked some pop girls about their kind of men.

Georgina Mells

Carroll Carter of Arrival looks for patience, humour and understanding in her ideal man. She says she is moody and he has to be able to put up with that. She likes masculine hands, narrow hips and domineering blokes. She also likes him to be a little crazy and so she chose *Spike Milligan* as a good example.

Other Arrival girl *Dyan Birch* likes men with tempers; she also likes men who are easygoing, daring, domineering, mad, un-muscley, and modern but not trendy. *Mick Jagger* has the right face, she says.

Actress *Fiona Lewis* would choose a man who was creative and funny and sexy and who knew how to enjoy himself. She thought that sounded like *Albert Finney.*

I always said that my Regal Reports should have been in hard back! Hiya darlins, yer ruler here about to mess up a page of this fabulous "Fab" album, feels quite posh writing for a real book!

Did you ever wonder what one disc-jockey thought of the next one? Well I haven't given it too much thought and that's probably because I get this pain in the head every time I think. Even so I withstood the pain for a number of minutes just so I could tell you what I think of some other Djs.

I don't know all the jocks personally but the ones I do know I'll tell you what I think of them as people as well as what I think of them professionally.

First off there's one of my longest standing mates and that's **Paul Burnett**. As an announcer he is the supreme professional, this is a feeling shared not only with his fans but with his bosses too. As a person, well of course I'm biased because he's my pal but I would much sooner spend an hour in his company than watch any of our top comedians.

He is most certainly one of the funniest men I know. He can impersonate absolutely anyone and if this huge talent of his isn't used in his future career then all I can say is what a great waste it will be!

A guy who often walks away with the award for the most popular disc-jockey in Great

Britain is **Tony Blackburn**, in my opinion these awards are well deserved. I first met Tony in 1965 when we compered a television show together. Later we worked on Radio Caroline together. I haven't seen him again since although I hear he's doing O.K. for himself.

As a person it would be impossible not to like him, that famous smile of his is very rarely off his face. These days poor old Tony is under that supercritical magnifying glass

REGAL REPORT

Being very chuffed at the idea of writing in a book, yer Regal Ruler gives his opinions of some of his fellow disc-jockeys.

which is always awaiting people who reach the top step on that fragile stairway to fame.

I think he does an excellent job, corny gags and all.

Bob Stewart is another old friend of mine. We sailed together on Caroline North and then dropped anchor together in Luxembourg. Bob takes life very seriously and because of this we often end up with a conversation dead-lock.

One of the finest qualities in a person is sincerity and this is something which Bob oozes.

John Peel is a person I have never met so there can be no saying what I think of him as a human being. As a disc jockey I think he is a nonentity, as a presenter of music I suppose he is adequate but my own personal feelings are that the people who are digging John's type of programme don't want a "personality" or flamboyant jock, therefore John does an excellent job. Even so I don't like this sort of approach personally in the same way that I am quite sure he doesn't dig yer Prince!

Emperor Rosko is one of the few people to influence my style of delivery. I worked with Rosko on Caroline South about the time when he had first come to our British shores. We had the same leave schedule together and stayed in the same hotel and, in fact, the same room.

Rosko is *the* Playboy and it took some keeping up with him I can tell you! He had, and probably still does, much more loot than me. Once whilst shopping for boots with him I

came out of the shop having ordered three pairs of made to measure boots clutching a bill for 48 gns! Rosko had ordered six pairs!

I'm quite sure that if Rosko could ask God to change any one thing he'd ask him to do away with sleep? A good friend to have, providing you could stick his pace. As a Dj I think him top of the class when it comes to doing a fast, tight all-go show. His show reflects his life!

Jimmy Young comes into my mind and I want him out of my mind as soon as possible! I can't imagine anything so boring as his programme.

I believe that uncountable Djs could do an even better job than he. The trouble is that no one else is given the chance to take his seat over for a few months.

As a person he's probably quite nice but I haven't met him so can't say and after what I've said I suppose I'd better hope that I don't meet him!

Kenny Everett is not a disc jockey! He's a first-class comedian who happens to insert his humour between

records. I met Kenny once whilst I was with "Caroline" and he "London", he gave me his phone number and said to ring him the next time I was in London so that we could have a night out. I still haven't got round to ringing him mainly because I've only been to London on fleeting and busy visits. Some day I'll ring him and ask him if he and Audrey would like that long promised night out with Christine and I! In the meantime I'll continue to admire him for the genius he is.

I must go in a minute cos I've got to write my Regal Report for next week's FAB but I must say how luverly it is been being in a book, very cozy! I can't go without saying **Dave Lee Travis** is a gas, we both wept on each other's shoulder the day we left Caroline for the last time! Daffy **Don Alan** is another old colleague of mine and he now works for Manx Radio on the Isle of Man. He is one of the cleverest Djs going with his "human" humour and if you holiday on this island take your trannie with you and don't you dare miss his shows!

Kid Jensen is the best pal a fella could have and I'm happy to have that honour. He's a laugh a minute although sometimes it's unintentional. To describe Kid in one word I would have to use the word "warm".

Keep warm.

Many loves and fanks for buying the first book I've been in, twant arf excitin'!

This is your own private page where you can list your own
personal records – away from prying eyes!

WEIGHT (list your pounds and stones on the 1st of each month)

J. .... A. .... Jy. .... O. ....

F. .... M. .... Aug. .... N. ....

M. .... J. .... S. .... D. ....

FAVE FLICKS (seen this year)
1. *Soldier Blue*
2. *Women in Love*
3. *Caroline*

DISTINGUISHED DISCS
1. *The Wedding*
2. ....
3. ....
4. ....

PLACE (the most exciting you visited. Paris maybe, or HIS home!)
....
....
....
....
....

GREATEST PERSONAL ACHIEVEMENT
(getting own front door key? Learning to swim?)
....
....
....

PEOPLE (the most interesting ones you met)
1. *My Future Hubby*
2. *Alistair*
3. ....
4. ....

BEST TV SHOWS
(your own nomination)
1. ....
2. ....
3. ....

BIG EVENT
(first time you flew? First time you tasted champagne?)
....
....

PRESENT
(the most wonderful gift you received) *Was my*
Engagement ring
given by *Alistair Milne*

Number of Birthday Cards received :

Number of Valentine Cards received :

Number of Christmas Cards received :

TOP SECRET

(Continued from page 37)

Shaming The Devil
By Derek Long

"I always told myself if I had an E-type I could pull myself a smashing bird as well. Today I sort of fell for the opportunity."

I thought that one over. So I was a smashing bird. I had no trouble at all in not feeling offended.

"You didn't have to tell me all this," I said to him, trying to keep my cool image still.

"That's me," he said. "Do something daft and then come clean. I'm no good at deceit."

That was nice. Who could like deceitful men? I felt a nasty little pang. What was I then? Just a deceitful girl. Not a smashing bird waiting to be pulled, but a little phoney.

"I expect you'll complain at the office," he said. "I wouldn't blame you. All I can say it was nice while it lasted. It was great. All I imagined it would be."

He looked at me and I looked at him.

"You're smiling," he said.

"That's right," I said. "And I'm not complaining."

"You're the greatest," he said. "I mean, a girl like you, I thought you'd give me hell."

"Why?"

"Girls like you tend to do that sort of thing," he said. "You meet 'em in my job. So thanks."

HE DROVE on and dropped me outside the office. We sat for a moment and looked at each other. I could see him thinking it over. I could practically read his mind.

Then I could see him deciding against it. I was the sort of girl who wanted to view thirteen thousand pound houses. And he wasn't the sort of boy who'd know a cheap little flash get-up, bought off the hook, if he saw it. To put it briefly, he just decided I was out of his bracket.

So he helped me out of the car, thanked me politely and drove off.

I went to the bus stop and waited. I felt awful. He'd told me the truth and I had all my shabby little pretences still weighing on my soul. I looked at my watch and saw it was nearly five o'clock.

I've mentioned it before, but I'm not without a little bit of cheek. This took some doing but I went back to the parking yard round the back of Carruthers and Son, Estate Agents.

It was easy to find. A shabby little open car with a tatty hood. It had Snoopy painted on the bonnet. The doors weren't locked, and I don't suppose the locks had worked in years.

There was only one place to wait—in Snoopy. So that's where I sat, and it was a quarter to six before he came.

He was quite speechless when he saw me there. So I said it first.

"Wouldn't you say this is more me than an E-type Jag?" I asked.

"I wouldn't dare," he said. "What brought you back here?"

"I'm like you," I told him. "I believe in telling the truth and shaming the devil. I've a confession to make as well."

So he got in beside me and I started to tell him.

I didn't know how he'd take it, but what other way was there of finding out?

THE END

©Derek Long 1970

WHOSE LITTLE GIRL ARE YOU? (see page 39)
These are the famous Dads (or Mums) of those pretty daughters. (How many did you get right?)

A. Talia, daughter of Davy Jones.

B. Kyoko, daughter of Anthony Cox (and Yoko Ono).

C. Catherine, daughter of Claude Wolff (and Petula Clark).

D. Samantha, daughter of Des O'Connor.

E. Sarah, daughter of Spencer Davis.

F. Victoria, daughter of Peter Sellers (and Britt Ekland).

G. Roberta, daughter of Bobby Moore.

H. Harriet, daughter of Noel Harrison.

I. Bindi, daughter of Rolf Harris.

J. Barbara-Michelle, daughter of Claude Wolff (and Petula Clark).

K. Mary, daughter of Paul McCartney.

L. Tracy, daughter of Des O'Connor.

M. Ami, daughter of Micky Dolenz.

N. Heather, daughter of Linda Eastman (now Mrs. Paul McCartney).

HAVE YOU GOT WHAT IT TAKES? (see page 9)

SCORE:

1. a – 2, b – 3, c – 1.
2. a – 1, b – 2, c – 3.
3. a – 2, b – 3, c – 2.
4. Score 2 for each "yes".
5. a – 3; b – 2, c – 1.
6. a – 2, b – 3, c – 1.
7. a – 1, b – 3, c – 1.
8. Score 4 for "yes" to any of them.
9. a – 1, b – 3, c – 2.
10. a – 1, b – 2, c – 4.
11. a – 3, b – 2, c – 0.
12. a – 1, b – 3, c – 4, d – 0.

RESULTS:

35 and over –
You have got what it takes and you probably know it, so spare a kindly thought for those who haven't, and start a second-hand man store!

20 to 30 –
You may not have been born with the necessary talents but you seem to have acquired them all right somewhere along the way. You're probably the luckiest category because you realise happy romances have to be worked on and don't take them for granted.

under 20 –
Oh dear! Perhaps you're just a bit slow on the uptake and maybe you'll meet the right man sooner or later, but it sounds as though it will be more chance than choice. Choose a vampish friend and pick up a few hints you can try for yourself.

Published by I.P.C. Magazines Ltd, Fleetway House, Farringdon Street, London E.C.4. Printed in England by W. S. Cowell Ltd, Butter Market, Ipswich. Sole Agents for Australia and New Zealand: Gordon & Gotch; South Africa: Central News Agency Ltd; Rhodesia: Zambia Kingstons Ltd.

76

AUTOGRAPH PARK

Here are the names of the well-known people who did the writing

1. The angular looped "t" bar shows persistence and sensitiveness. The medium-large writing indicates a person who gets down to fundamentals, prefers action to reflection.

2. Signs of absentmindedness, but the looped letters show a sensitive, even touchy nature. The open letter "a" shows generosity. A keen mind and gentle personality.

3. The angular plain "A" indicates an artist or writer, and a lover of animals. Emotional and sensitive with a good deal of imagination but an idealistic nature.

4. This angular hand points to an exacting, often demanding person who hasn't a good sense of humour. He concentrates best under pressure.

5. The sweeping loop of the "g" indicates a person with strong primitive impulses. Responds to jazz and rhythmical music as he does to sex.

6. Signs of impulsiveness and enthusiasm. This is an artistic hand but not the hand of a dreamer. A sensitive person, but a person who likes to get things done.

7. This is very rhythmical writing but there is a lazy tendency in this person's nature. The many loops show generosity.

8. This is the writing of a highly efficient, clear-thinking person. A person of strong opinions, not afraid to make decisions, with faith in his own judgement.

9. The round appearance and breaks in the writing show signs of immaturity. Also signs of a good judge of character, not bent on impulsiveness.

10. This is not the hand of a sensitive person, nor emotional. This is a person of commonsense, good judgement, regularity, giving way sometimes to an artistic streak.

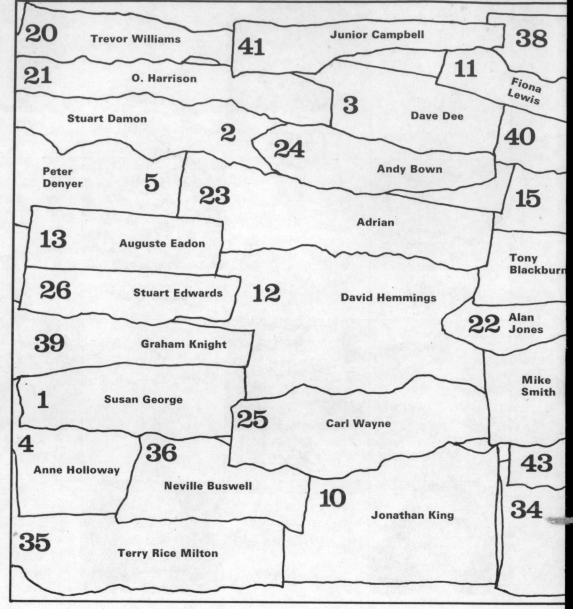

14. I see traces of impulsiveness, a touchy nature and a person who easily takes offence. No real great ambitions.

15. The writer is not sure of himself or his feelings, but in material things is precise. The plain "P" and "I" show he sticks to essentials.

16. The flamboyant hand is a sign of egotism, but also originality. Not a very emotional person, but the hand of an artist.

17. Again the plain "I" shows a desire to stick to essentials. Likes to contemplate. A person who

likes to think his word is final.

18. Materialistic, likes decisions to be made and no hanging about. The open "a" is a sign of generosity where emotions are involved, and talkative.

19. Generous nature shown by letters open at the top. Flamboyancy shows he is versatile, with slight signs of vanity, but also originality.

20. Interested in people and a gay social life. The high-flying dot of the "i" shows high-flying

thoughts, slightly irresponsible. Impulsive.

21. Likes to dream and has a few fantasies in life. No great zest or ambition in life. The final letters dwindling into mere strokes indicate shrewdness.

22. The "t" bar that roofs the word shows a spirit of protection, could be patronising to some people. Artistic hand, slightly egotistic, and likes to have the final word.

23. A lover of colour, rhythm and music. Tendency to generous ges-

11. The open letter "a" shows this person is generous. Slightly impulsive and a great enthusiasm about many things is indicated by the dot way ahead of the "i".

12. The hooks over the "i" show a sense of humour. There are signs of great physical energy. The writer is probably materialistic with an artistic side to his nature.

13. This person thinks logically, is not apt to act impulsively. An artistic streak is trying to release itself, but the steadier side of the character dominates.